INSURGENT RAIN

Selected Poems 1974–1996

Rienzi Crusz

Selected and Introduced by
Chelva Kanaganayakam

TSAR
Toronto
1997

We acknowledge the support of the Canada Council for the Arts for our publishing program. We also acknowledge support from the Ontario Arts Council.

Cover art by Mrinal Mitra.

Canadian Cataloguing in Publication Data

Crusz, Rienzi, 1925-
   Insurgent rain : selected poems 1974–1996

ISBN 0-920661-67-X

I. Kanaganayakam, C. (Chelvanayakam), 1952–
II. Title.
PS8555.R87I56 1997   C811'.54   C97-931719-3
PR9199.3.C72I56 1997

Printed in Canada by Coach House Printing.

TSAR Publications
P. O. Box 6996, Station A
Toronto, Ontario M5W 1X7
Canada

BOOKS BY RIENZI CRUSZ

Flesh and Thorn
Elephant and Ice
Singing Against the Wind
A Time for Loving
Still Close to the Raven
The Rain Doesn't Know Me Any More
Beatitudes of Ice

NOTE TO THIS EDITION

In the poems selected for this edition, spellings, hyphenation and capitalization have been standardized and made uniform in consultation with the author. Each poem is followed by a citation to the book in which it appears or is indicated "new," as the case may be. In addition, some of the poems have also undergone minor alterations by the author. The following abbreviations have been used for the titles of the author's previous books.

FT	*Flesh and Thorn*
EI	*Elephant and Ice*
SW	*Singing Against the Wind*
TL	*A Time for Loving*
SR	*Still Close to the Raven*
RD	*The Rain Doesn't Know Me Any More*
BI	*Beatitudes of Ice*

Contents

The Igloo of Heaven

The Umbrella of Doting Children

A New Architecture

These Other Configurations

Soul of a Faltering Saint

Introduction

One can hardly miss the ironies inherent in the title of Rienzi Crusz's most recent collection of poems, *Beatitudes of Ice* (1995), or for that matter in the poet's decision to conclude this book with a poem that pays homage to a long line of poets who have in various ways influenced his writing. While Crusz has, in occasional poems and more specifically in his rare critical essay "Talking for Myself" that appeared in *The Toronto South Asian Review*, drawn attention to his indebtedness to British, European and Latin American poets, it is in that concluding poem that he acknowledges most fully the multiple traditions from which he gained both insight and formal sophistication. In it there is little "anxiety of influence" (to use Harold Bloom's phrase), and no self-consciousness about the politics of colonialism and "mainstream literature"; there is simply a frank admission of what it means to become a poet writing in English. The "drumbeat of Avon," the "psalms of David," the "melody" of Dylan and the songs of "good Manley" are all part of the process of learning "how to dance in this rarefied air" (*Beatitudes* 67–68). The poem thus stresses that whatever turns and twists his poetic career took over three decades, whatever poetic and political stances he adopted as a result of private and public circumstances, he has felt the need to differentiate between poetics and ideology, even if it meant reconciling two agonistic worldviews in the interests of his vocation.

If, however, among these diverse influences, one were to single out a particularly significant tradition—one that exerted the greatest force on his sensibility—it would probably be the poetry of Romanticism, particularly in its emphasis on the primacy of the imagination, the celebration of emotion and passion, and in its attitude to the benevolence of nature. Echoes of Modernism do appear in his poetry, particularly in the poems that establish an ironic distance from his subject matter or those that work with metaphors to displace and objectify an emotionally charged experience; but the consistent attraction has been to the kind of lyric that gives expression to the power of emotion and sentiment, even when it borders on sentimentality or hyperbole. It is a quality that Irving Layton, among others, recognized early in his writing as an attribute that sets him apart from

ix

the majority of contemporary Canadian poets, and one which Reshard Gool, in his introduction to *A Time for Loving* (1986), stresses repeatedly as a distinctive trait. As Gool puts it, "the verse rehearses grand risks, invention, resource" (vii). The much-earlier *Flesh and Thorn* (1974)—which, appropriately, chooses for its epigraph Sappho's "Love with his gift of pain"—is almost exclusively concerned with the exploration of passion, often in its allusion to one

who once set fire to wet grass
with torches in your limbs,
coaxed suns like butterflies
on to your open palms,
spoke words as passionate
as elephant trumpeting the moon.

("Pardon My Muted Ways," *Flesh*, n.p.)

The preoccupation with love, in all its facets but particularly passion, beauty, betrayal and despair, and with nature that both reflects and transforms subjective states, is hardly surprising since so much of his early poetry is linked with the personal circumstances that compelled his emigration to Canada.

Crusz was born in Sri Lanka (then known as Ceylon) into a middle-class, conservative, Burgher family in 1925, and grew up in Colombo, where he had his education at St Peter's College and later at the University of Ceylon where he read history. Whatever training in and exposure to English literature he had was gained from his father's library and from his brother Hilary, who later became a well-known zoologist and scientist, rather than from any formal training. He speaks candidly about this period of his life in "Talking for Myself" and insists that he came to "English on his own terms," which explains the absence of any juvenilia in his work. When, after a period of postgraduate training in England in library science, he returned to Sri Lanka in 1953, radical changes were beginning to take place in the newly independent nation and what seemed like a long and prestigious career as a librarian at the Central Bank was cut short, partly due to the changes in the political climate of a country committed to active decolonization but more specifically due to the breakdown of his marriage and the "raging chaos of love" that accompanied the departure of his wife. Very much a result of this desertion, his early poetry became a recollection of how "she rose like a zombie/and walked into her beloved Night" (*Flesh*, "Little Brown Boy," n.p.). Following the collapse of his marriage, he too then left the country in 1965, with his three children, to begin a new life in Canada, a decision that becomes the subject of his unpublished children's story "Bumpis, the Magic Elephant." If the relative stability of life in Canada and the passage of time have both assuaged the pain of betrayal and deflected the focus of his poetry, he has nonetheless remained very much the poet of passion, creating poems that, as Uma Parameswaran claims, go "singing into Canadian literature to the sound of Kandyan drums" (153).

If the sheer momentum and energy of lines such as,

And when like a bird
stoned in magnificent flight
I hurtled down, down
among dogs and flowers and kings,
their karmic tongues did not speak,
the Buddha eyes did not weep. . .

("The Sun-Man Looks at Pain," *Flesh*, n.p.)

has now given way to a much mellower and controlled poetry that is more reflective and more subtle in its evocation of moods, the impulse to work with emotion is as strong as ever. In the love poems written to his wife Anne, the poems that describe his children, and even those in which the sun-man encounters racism, the imaginative and the passionate are still constitutive aspects. In an unpublished poem entitled "Libra" he rehearses his own death, with a defiance that recalls Blake and intertextually connects with Dylan Thomas:

No. I will not "go gently into that dark night"
you'll first hear
the Kandyan drums make fire
under the dancer's anklet bells,
the raven caw the breaking news,
the elephant's last clear trumpet . . .

But Crusz's reputation as a Sri Lankan or hyphenated Canadian poet has been a result not of his love poetry or his elegiac lyrics but of those that deal with migrancy, with his status in Canada as an immigrant poet. Crusz's second collection *Elephant and Ice* (1980) has probably been the most influential in foregrounding the immigrant theme, although the notion of exile has never been far from his consciousness. "Elephant" and "Ice" have served as tropes in positioning his "public" self in a literary climate where ethnicity is a source of endless debate. In addition to the duality of these two images, the persona of the "sun-man," "winter man" and "raven," all of which the poet assumes to explore different facets of the migrant experience, serve as markers for relating the experience of living on the cusp of alienation, racism, identity and nostalgia. Despite his reservations about the ethnic label that defines his poetry and his identity, Crusz himself has courted this image with a substantial body of poems that move from one end of the spectrum of migration to the other, celebrating, critiquing and ironizing these two worlds. In "Elegy for the Sun-man's Children Going" he speaks of "This immigrant poet,/whose road was never his, but went" (*Elephant*, 28) and in "Dark with Excessive Bright" he admits: "Dark I am/and darkly do I sing" (*Elephant* 90), all of which point to his own insistent concern with being an outsider in Canada.

The binaries in themselves are significant, and they find expression in the sensuous imagery of flowers, fruits and the beauty of nature in Sri Lanka, as against the cold, the snow and the bleakness of Canada. On the one hand the sun-man remembers

> how he once lived;
> on a fistful of rice,
> shred of dried fish,
> mango and pineapple,
> coconut milk dripping
> from his mouth . . .   (*Elephant*, 20)

On the other, in an alien land, the sun-man crawls

> into his sun-dial nerves
> and sleeps
> with myths and shibboleths
> as central heating steals
> under his dark eyelids   (*Elephant*, 35)

If an awareness of the disparity between these two worlds and the predicament of exile are essential to any reading of Crusz, the emphasis on duality to the exclusion of an indeterminate middle ground has been both productive and frustrating. If the critical material about his exilic sensibility has served the function of establishing Crusz as a major "multicultural" writer, it has also had the consequence of obscuring the complexities of experience and of formal invention that frame his writing. Migrancy has thus been a mixed blessing, one which has brought him recognition in certain quarters as a poet who gives expression to the immigrant consciousness, and alienation in others as one who locates himself outside mainstream concerns.

Arun Mukherjee, for instance, has in several articles consistently referred to Crusz's capacity to reveal "what it is to be an immigrant and a non-white in a society that is so dissimilar from that of one's origin" (21) and praises the manner in which he negotiates the politics of otherness. Mukherjee sees in Crusz's writing the opposite of the impulses that run through Michael Ondaatje's poetry, which lack commitment to the social and political realities of Sri Lanka and foreground the aesthetic at the expense of the referential. Mukherjee is emphatic about her own standards that require literature to "say something" and within that paradigm Crusz succeeds where Ondaatje doesn't. While such formulations tend to imply a wholly tendentious bent in one and a belletristic impulse in the other, Crusz himself makes a distinction between the two in a poem called "Going for Broke" where he affirms his penchant for "batik profusion."

In contrast to the views of Mukherjee, Craig Tapping in a review of *A Time for Loving* that appeared in *Canadian Literature* has been sceptical of the poet's handling of the dualities of home and exile and sees in Crusz a "colonial's dangerous nostalgia" (147). For Tapping, Crusz is very much the essentialist whose recreation of "home" is a form of appropriation. Along similar lines, but in greater detail, Suwanda Sugunasiri takes to task all Sri Lankan poets writing in Canada for their lack of commitment, their distance from the realities of the country they left behind. For Sugunasiri, the differences between Ondaatje and Crusz are less important than the fact they both "fled the revolution" of Sri Lanka and have thus become self-imposed outsiders. For him Crusz is "no closer to being Sinhalese or Sri Lankan than Ondaatje, in his sensibility or rootedness" (67).

In a literary climate that is increasingly sensitive to the nuances of otherness, it is hardly surprising that the positioning of Crusz has become a matter of concern. Notions of essentialism, authenticity, appropriation and nostalgia are often invoked to celebrate or discredit the author's stance. While individual poems can be cited to prove one point or another, what is often inadequately recognized is the manner in which the poems resonate against each other to produce intersections that resist any easy taxonomy.

Andrew Stubbs is right in his observation that "the range of contrasts" in Crusz's poetry "narrate the endlessly repeating history of his journey from Ceylon to Canada" (1)—a retelling of the process of displacement. But it is also a narration that is constantly in a state of flux as the poet moves from the referential to the reflective, from the lyrical to the narrative, from celebration to acceptance. The shifts in persona counterpoint the fixity suggested by the pronominal "I" to explore shades of meaning, the uncertainties of Keats's "negative capability." If "the white silence of civilization" is stifling in one poem, the beauty of the burning bush is enough "to bring another Moses to his knees" (*Beatitudes*, 12) in another. This "white marshmallow land" is both his and not his. If, as he desires in a recent poem called "Love Poem for Anne #4" to

> tell the raven and the elephant
> that I still sing their extravagant song,
> parade their metaphors
> without compromise

and demonstrate that his sense of loss is undiminished, he is also conscious of the violence in the country, and speaks

> about Colombo's walking dead
> the suicide-bombers, the blood
> that flows so freely in the dusty North

and about the changes that have transformed the nation. Canada is still not home, but it is an "igloo of heaven" where he is at home and, as he remarks in another poem, he is

> [a] brown laughing face
> in the snow,
> not the white skull
> for the flies
> in Ceylon's deadly sun.   (*Elephant*, 95)

The ostensible binaries can be deceptive in Crusz's work and, as he points out in his wonderful poem "Roots," his own identity, marked by hybridity, defies the easy dichotomies of East and West. Of his Burgher (i.e. Eurasian) ancestry and his ambiguous status in Sri Lanka, he says:

> A Portuguese captain holds
> the soft brown hand of my Sinhala mother.
> It's the year 1515 AD,
> when two civilizations kissed and merged,
> and I, Burgher of that hot embrace,
> write a poem of history . . .   (*Singing*, 42)

The syncretism does not invalidate the fondness with which the poet recalls the Sri Lankan landscape or uses it to contrast the bleakness of Canada, but he is aware of the ambivalence of his own inheritance. The colonial legacy is a complex one, clearly oppressive and hegemonic, as the rulers exploited the land and its people. He recalls

> [h]ow your freighters coughed black,
> then guffawed and left heavy
> with coconut and tea,
> cardamom, cinnamon and ivory.   (*Rain*, 2)

And yet, having learnt the language, the poet is inevitably a part of that tradition. In a context where decolonization and "writing back" are axiomatic, Crusz has consistently expressed this sense of divided loyalty. Quite rightly, Michael Thorpe sees him in relation to an older generation of postcolonial writers who could "appropriate the colonial legacy of Shakespeare and English without anguished breast-beating. . ." (130).

The land he left behind is where his ancestral memory resides, and the allegiance is rendered complex by his own Burgher status. He is an immigrant poet, but one for whom the cusp between worlds is both loss and gain. The challenge for him has been to create a system of mythology that transcends the referential and brings together the primordial relation to the land he has left. If the image clusters that make up this elaborate system have been mistaken for gestures of essentialism, it is at least partly because the fictive has been confused with the referential. Images of the elephant and the raven are part of the natural world that the poet alludes to, and they are part of the landscape he remembers, but his use of them as markers for the subconscious and the mythical is what gives to his poems their particular texture. It is the interplay of the real and the fictive that leads for instance, to the claim:

When the raven talks
listen,
it is God
in ultimate disguise.   (*Rain*, 44)

Here the raven in its referential mode is the other, the voice of the margins that is the target of discrimination. But the raven is also part of a mystical world, the symbol of a religious consciousness and the voice of God. Crusz is always conscious that language creates its own reality and if what is offered as the real is no more than a fictive construct, it is because his poetry rejects the various closures that ideological commitment demands.

It is hardly an accident that Derek Walcott appears time and again as an intertextual reference in Crusz's poetry. At its most obvious both share an awareness of racial mixture that flaunts hybridity; more significantly, they reveal a scepticism about nationalist narratives that employ a unitary model to legitimize a particular ideology. In both one sees a denunciation of the hegemony of colonialism and a celebration of the language that the rulers left behind. The self-reflexivity that surfaces constantly in Crusz's poetry is a reminder that at some level his concern is with language, with the power of metaphor not merely to reflect but also to shape experience. The large number of poems that are explicitly self-referential is again an indication that for Crusz the relation between the fictive and the referential is hardly ever simple or straightforward.

Singing Against the Wind (1985), Crusz's third volume of poetry, begins with a poem entitled "The Elephant Who Would Be a Poet," which serves as an apologia for his poetry and as an illustration of the various preoccupations that run through his work. It is an example of the short, carefully structured, tonally perfect, witty and meditative poem that he often writes and is comfortable with. While it makes perfect sense as a stand-alone poem with its internal coherence and its formal structure, it is also part of a larger system of images—a private mythology—that he creates to anchor his ideas and give them resonance. The elephant, apart from its referential function in relation to the event described in the poem, serves also as a symbol of the landscape that the poet has left behind and that has been a shaping influence in his poetic career.

"The Elephant Who Would Be a Poet" is a poem about the process of writing poetry, about the isolation of the poet and his alienation from those around him, told through the image of the elephant and the mahout. After a day of tiring and monotonous logging, the elephant decides to relax in a most unusual manner:

> Without command
> he eases his huge body to the ground,
> rolls over,
> makes new architecture
> from his thick legs,
> four columns vertical
> to the sun.

Predictably, the mahout is taken by surprise and is confused by the display of dissent:

> The confused mahout
> refuses the poem
> in this new equilibrium,
> this crazy theatre of the mind . . .   (*Singing*, 9)

This, then, is the role of the poet—the outsider, the person who sees things differently and acts unconventionally, much to the annoyance and incomprehension of the reader who would prefer to see the poet in a much more conventional role. In different ways, the need to define his craft and his own concerns become, inevitably, a central concern in all his published volumes. Rather than lead to self-indulgence and posturing, this self-reflexivity enables the poet to look at himself with ironic detachment, as in another poem in which his son Michael wonders, "What's so hot about dad's poetry?" (*Singing*, 68) and the poet, with characteristic self-awareness, admits that there is nothing particularly new "about this immigrant theme," and wonders why he chooses to flaunt it like a side of beef. While the convention of poets reflecting on their poetry is hardly new, its urgency and relevance for Crusz, who is sharply conscious of his hyphenated status, can hardly be underestimated.

In another poem, a reader is enticed by the pervasive "elephant image" and decides to give a "tiny crystal elephant" as a Christmas gift to the poet, thereby transforming the metaphoric into the metonymic. Wanting to pursue the relation between symbol and substance, the poet probes further about the friend's response to his poetry and is told to look again at the crystal elephant. He does, and "a very lopsided beast/was staring back at him with curious eyes" (*Beatitudes*, 57). Removed from the larger system of which it is a part, the beast looks awkward and exoticized, the symbol at once inappropriate, comic and irrelevant. Time and again the poetry is an affirmation and subversion of various stances. If the poet is defiant and serious in one, he is dismissive and humorous in another as he goes through various stages of introspection. There is hardly any finality, any closure, only a constant quest for a mode that would be both a narrative of a complex journey and a stay against the vicissitudes occasioned by the journey. The natural process of growth and decay concerns him and becomes the subject of his poetry. But he is equally concerned with the aesthetic, the capacity to detach the experience from its subjectivity to explore in metaphor the artistic appeal of the moment. Hence, the description of the mango leaf:

> Now, cleanly autumned, scarlet,
> at the feet of its mother tree,
> with the sun veiling its small architecture
> like a tabernacle,
> and the tree smiling at its roots
> for a death
> so exotically done.　　　　　　　(*Elephant*, 52)

The self-reflexivity and the introspection are at least in part a consequence of a genuine concern with his own predicament of living on the cusp, of negotiating two worlds, of being anxious about his own directions. They also draw attention to all the areas of experience—the cosmic scheme—that occupy him. Very little attention has been paid, for instance, to all the poems devoted to his family, to his parents and his brother and to "the umbrella of doting children." In the poems devoted to his parents one finds a quality of unreserved adulation. If these poems in their concern with the narrative element sometimes lack the sensuous metaphoric dimension of his other poems, they still do occupy a central place in his work. And they shed light on the peculiar paradox of how despite a country that spurned him and a wife who deserted him, he still retains a profound sense of attachment to the land.

Some of the earliest poems published by Crusz in *Grail* have been about religion, no doubt inspired by his own convictions and his strong Catholic background. As early as in *Elephant and Ice* (59,66) Christian mythology and imagery resonate in his poems, and that is consistent with his education at a Christian school and his own admiration for Milton and Hopkins. However, the didactic poems which parade a religious sentiment are sometimes the least effective. Thus the tendentious edge of "Sermon in the Forest" reinforces the conventionality of the poem. Where the religious impulses come into contact (and conflict) with a secular imagination, the poems take on a richly textured and multiplicitous quality. A case in point is the first stanza of "The Gardener," which reads:

> Since Adam
> had fouled things up
> by trying to live under God
> with a naked woman, a serpent,
> and an apple tree,
> this gardener's ambition
> was to remake Eden
> in only a garden of roses.   (*Flesh*, n.p.)

In poetry that is as reminiscent of John Donne and Herbert Vaughn as it is of Indian *bhakti* poetry, Crusz demonstrates a resistance to any easy taxonomy. Religion becomes the occasion for satire, for exuberant wit, for the exposure of deep-seated hypocrisy and racism and for philosophical speculation about theology. "The Accepted One" remains a particularly important poem, written on the occasion of his brother's decision to give up priesthood, and ending with the reassuring thought,

> Father Magee opened
> a small door
> into a cockeyed world,
>
> and God did not pitch the sun
> with dark thoughts.   (*Still*, 69)

The tradition of *bhakti* poetry becomes clearer in those poems that adopt a tone of irreverence, of playful banter, of infusing a childlike innocence into what is ostensibly a religious poem. If in "Yes, in Our

Father's House There Are Many Rooms" the gesture of asking God for a room and then a bungalow for his family satirizes the materialism of institutionalized religion, it also reflects that liberty and that deep sense of conviction associated with the best of *bhakti* literature.

It is tempting and perhaps not altogether wrong to offer a teleological view of Crusz's evolution as a poet. The very first volume is, as Uma Parameswaran and several others have observed, deeply personal, concerned for the most part with private sorrows and the struggle of living in an alien land, and the second volume is concerned with the two worlds of Sri Lanka and Canada and the trials faced by the poet who attempts to make the transition. It is here that one becomes conscious of the various binaries that later came to be associated with his oeuvre. *Singing Against the Wind*, as the title suggests, is about forms of resistance, about the need to go against the grain. The subsequent volumes are at once an assertion that the poet is still close to that world, despite the changes wrought by time, and an admission of the complexity of identifying "home"—of being nourished and abandoned by the rain. In *Beatitudes*, there is a greater affinity with the new home, a greater willingness to accept both worlds as essential to the poet. As Shyam Selvadurai rightly points out in a recent review, "suddenly the notion of his foreignness, his yearning for Sri Lanka are undercut and one is aware of a life lived, a history made here; a sense of belonging in spite of oneself" (25).

Such an evolutionary scheme serves as a defence against the notion that the poet's career has hardly evolved in the last two decades. It reveals a certain change of thematic emphasis in his writing. The taxonomy is convenient but it suggests a trajectory of growth and evolution that is hardly accurate. In fact something of the raw power of his earlier poetry is hardly ever captured in the more mellow and meditative later work. And there is a cyclical pattern in his poetry, a tendency to go back to themes that need to be expressed again. If a linear pattern is a necessary route for the reader, so is a synchronic one that draws attention to repetitive structures that inform his work. Hence the logic of the present collection, which favours the synchronic over the diachronic.

To pay attention to the linear narrative of home and exile is to chart the complex journey of a poet who has moved from the personal to the public and from despair and pessimism to reconciliation and acceptance. In fact, that would substantiate the emphasis of his poem "Homecomings," which speaks about

the journey's throbbing walk
to this igloo of heaven
or that sun-faced island of the elephant
where I'm always at home,
if not home.

But Crusz's claim to serious recognition lies not simply in the various stances, not even in the range of subject matter, but in the manner in which the poems relate to each other and resonate to create meaning and draw attention to themselves. What the image of the elephant communicates in one poem is complemented, subverted, questioned and built on in another. If the poet's birth is associated with Libra in one poem, that itself becomes the subject of another work and the promise of one poem is fulfilled in another.

The centripetal focus established by the network of imagery strengthens the rhythmic dimension of his poetry. Hardly a formalist, Crusz has written few poems that recapitulate established metrical forms. But the sonnet, the heroic couplet, the ballad and a whole range of stanzaic patterns are constant echoes in his free verse forms where each line and each stanza reflects that consciousness of metrical patterns in a manner that is unusual in contemporary poetry. While the minimalist poem, that highly condensed expression of experience, is not altogether unusual in his corpus, his strength lies in the more expansive mode where the line lengths, the enjambment, the counterpointing of metrical patterns, and the unfailing attention to the oral quality of poetry make his poetry striking in their appeal. Even when the subject matter is overtly tendentious as in "Faces of the Sun-man" one is struck by the sure sense of rhythm and the symbiotic relation between metaphor and prosody.

When Michael Thorpe, in a review of Crusz's *The Rain Doesn't Know Me Any More* makes the grand assertion that Crusz is "arguably the best living Sri Lankan poet in English" (130), the claim is neither perfunctory nor casual. The comparison that the comment implies is an important one which brings into focus a number of poets writing in Sri Lanka, Australia and North America. Thorpe's comment establishes Crusz's ongoing concern with the Sri Lankan scene. Equally true is the poet's dialogue with the Canadian scene, where he is both marginal and mainstream, at odds with the restrictive conventions that label him as the other, and perfectly at home in the tradition of the sensuous lyric.

WORKS CITED

Crusz, Rienzi. "Talking for Myself." *The Toronto South Asian Review* 6.1 (1987): 29-35.

Gool, Reshard. Introduction. *A Time for Loving*. By Rienzi Crusz. Toronto: TSAR, 1986. vii–x.

Mukherjee, Arun. "Songs of an Immigrant: The Poetry of Rienzi Crusz." *Currents* 4.1 (1986/87): 19-21.

Parameswaran, Uma. "The Singing Metaphor: Poetry of Rienzi Crusz." *Canadian Literature* 132 (Spring 1992): 146-54.

Selvadurai, Shyam. Review of *Beatitudes of Ice*. *Books in Canada* 25.5 (1996): 25.

Stubbs, Andrew. "Keeping Iago: Rituals of Innocence In Rienzi Crusz's Recent Poetry." (Unpublished)

Sugunasiri, Suwanda HJ. "'Sri Lankan' Canadian Poets: The Bourgeoisie that Fled the Revolution." *Canadian Literature*, 132 (Spring 1992): 60-79.

Tapping, Craig. "Front Lines." Review of *A Time for Loving*, by Rienzi Crusz. *Canadian Literature* 117 (Summer 1988): 145-47.

Thorpe, Michael. Review of *The Rain Doesn't Know Me Any More*. *World Literature Today* 68.1 (1994): 130.

The Raging Chaos of Love

Taste of Old Wine

After ten years
on replay
in slow motion
the way
she killed me off

seems clean
and surgical
a poem
spilling
from the tongue
of the jewelled cobra

The spring moment
when I searched
her eyes, jumped
the cool mercury
to summer pitch

she slowly turned
her polished head
caught me
in pale blue gun sights
and gently squeezed
the trigger

At the time
it was sound
and lightning pain
of whiplash
blue shrapnel
demanding silence

All along
she knew
the ways of flowers   *FT*

3

How Does One Reach the Sweet Kernel?

The way
the Ceylonese farmer
husks the coconut:
a crowbar planted
in the ground,
and the iron tooth
jabs the skin;
the flesh tears
till the bone shows
round and clean;
the hammer of machete
on the skull,
the milk leaks
and the sweet kernel opens out
like a womb.

For the kind of love
that hangs exotic and hard
like a bunch of king coconuts
on the palm of our dreams,
we need to tear the pink fibres
on our crowbar nerves,
machete the shell
of stubborn eyes
and burst into the kernel
of the heart.

Gentility,
the warm tentative hand
will only do
in the kind of love that shares
the breed of plums.   FT

Ceylon(ese): former name for Sri Lanka(ns)

Autograph Album

On that first blue page,
her mother writes (with letters
that tilt wildly,
    "Be good, sweet maid
    And let who will be clever"
    Love—Mom.

A favourite uncle:
    "Be good, sweetie.
    Always follow the constant sun,
    not the loafing ways
    of the moon."
    Love—Uncle Matthew.

Pages turn pink, white, yellow,
as words and autographs fall
like warm sweet rain:

    "Take care, pretty face"— Love, Joe

    "May all your dreams come true"—
    Your best friend, Margie
    "Love all, but choose only one"
    — Secret Admirer . . .

I gaze into her big brown eyes,
searching
the heart's intricate pathways,
for a love to outlast
time's cruel betrayals.

So, I recall the Bard:
    "This above all
    to thine own self be true,
    and as night follows the day
    Thou shalt be false to no man."
    Always, with love—Rienzi

Time. You once cantered
like our new love,
through those beginning years,
then lingered around
for fifteen,
an oracle that somehow never spoke.

Where were you in the ravaging end?
Why those strange silences
when dark prophecies
were in full bloom?
Do I have to sing
of how truth festered and died
under your watch,
of the mouth that would not speak
with the poet's true voice:

"Love, not death is the bitter thing."

New

Biography of an Elusive Cat

Nothing to go on,
date of birth or pedigree,
I write biography
from paw marks,
stray hairs on my shoulder,
a trace of Persian smell
somewhere round my thighs.

She came in
          unannounced,
from nowhere under stars,
wearing rich furs.
Moves like a thin flame,

my eye in vertigo

unable to settle
whether she flaunts
a blue ash or ash blue,
like water changing its skin
with sun and shadow.

Refuses
          to be held
in the still stance of stone,
turns my eyeball
on her fur thighs
ever moving, flowing
with oil in the joints.

Eludes
          the embracing fire
in my hands, an art
of sliding like cold cobra
through grass fingers.
Allows me only
                    to clutch
and hold her erotic purring.
And yet,
she was always there,
a presence, Persian aura
hung like an amulet
over my loins,

or like a river
holding me down
in her soft bed,
wrapping my legs
with exotic waters,
still escaping, chasing
the deep sea current.
The night she disappeared,
the neighbours said
as soon as the moon

hung its burnished head
on the cadju-pulang tree,
they thought they heard
the thin purring of leaves,
saw a warm shadow
                    flowing
into the night,
with something like a tail on fire
high in the wind.

FT

cadju-pulang: cashew nut, which hangs from a fleshy fruit

The Night Before My Birthday

The dream
went something like this:
in a naked house, white,
breathing the smell of Dettol,
like an empty ward
with its mouth open
for the coming of the lame and the limp.

My Spanish furniture,
pictures, poetry books, all gone:
the flight
        of velvet drapes,
        warm dust of trivia,
        forty-four years of matured griefs,
        red joys that burned in dark corners,
and the smell of children
                            scraped out
by some detergent hand.

My ex-wife crawls,

a fluid limbo dancer,
from under the slit of door:
all rags, her face caked like a ghost,
she asks: where are the children?
Fled, fled, I cry,
Noah's doves seek the olive branch.
And the gods of Kataragama
bleed in their shrines
as a whiff of frangipani
curls through the antiseptic air
and disappears.

And I am born
into my forty-fifth year
with the taunt of warm fires
                              burnt out,
faces of children   lost
in the jungle of new apartments,
old scars
            hurting like wounds,

the raging chaos of love.

FT

kataragama: A famous "pilgrim" village in Sri Lanka

9

For Daphne

Once I had all,
and all was the olive skin
warmed in the sun,
eyes black as hell
and ravens nesting in your hair.
Love, safe as a foetus,
happy and dancing at the end
of an umbilical cord.

Then you were born
with an alien rib of stone,   *ref. to Adam & Eve.*
some other bitter sap of soul,
reaching for another wind,
clawing the air
about your wet ears,
until finally
you found your tempest.

And I saw
the sun eyes dissolve,
thin strands of hair
blow like leaves
your temple bell raped   *body. self.*
of its golden tongue,
and silence staring
from a nameless face.
That day,
I stood alone
and felt the thunder of your blood
merge with the morning sun.
Now every morning,
I see the sun preach this other face,
I hear the splintering of mirrors
in my empty red house.

FT

full realization of abandonment + indifference or dislike of the other (wife?). bitter.

10

The Gardener

Since Adam
had fouled things up
by trying to live under God
with a naked woman, a serpent,
and an apple tree,
this gardener's ambition
was to remake Eden
in only a garden of roses.

He would tell the story
of his labours
through lean dark years
in the grief of scars
on his thick knuckles,
his calloused palms
where dirt had churned
the beginning of flowers.

When God's hot breath
finally broke rain,
and roses exploded
under his disciplined eyes,
he still couldn't claim
an Eden before the apple,

I can't undo things. start again completely new. past is irrevocable.

for one wild sunflower rose,
seeded unknown
in his boundaries of perfection,
cheating his guillotine of weeds,
now reared her saffron head
and cried: Pick me,
and I'll sing you a song
of first love.

As the sunflower petals
teased through his fingers,

each falling
like small symmetrical suns
at his feet, echoes of childhood games:
I love you, I love you not,
I love you, I love you not.

The rim of soft fire
now almost undone,
the last petal throbbing
like a dark exotic woman
in his arms, softly breathing:
I love you, I love you,
I am Eden, before, after, and now.

FT

Little Brown Boy

For John

For six years now
I've watched you turn winter
into a magnificent gambol:
flinging your snowballs
with deadly accuracy,
cutting rhythms, figurines,
with knives under your shoes.
Blood of the sun
still itching in your skin,
ice on fire, fire on ice,
you shape a predictable carnival.

Nor have you lost
those Singhala ears
that like the elephant
hear the wood apple fall

gentle as a raindrop
on the sleeping lotus;
it's the glow in your eyes
at birdsong under snow,
or the drumbeat of ice.

Not knowing
where your father
collected his wounds or how,
not smelling temple flowers,
red jambu wet
on rain-fresh trees,
you miss nothing, free
from your history's pain.

I think you're ready now
for some bulletin
from a night long ago:
when cats wailed
on the parapet wall,
and the wind called,
called through the na trees,
and she rose like a zombie
and walked into her beloved night.

And you slept on,
defying
   emptiness
closing my silent wound,

knowing all.

FT

Singhala (or Sinhala): the major ethnic group in Sri Lanka
wood apple: applelike fruit with a hard shell
temple flower: A white flower used in Buddhist temples
jambu: red, cherrylike fruit
na tree: a large fruit tree

Karma

The going away in June
was cruel. I see the gull
flee the salty spray
and linger on the wet rock
with the fading smell
of frangipani.

Purple grape
crushes in the black hands,
havocks in the heart.
The empty space shaped
to the slim body mocking
the bleeding eyes,
the nerves stretch along
the fluid horizon.

How the eye turns,
the mind shifts,
and the hills stir
to the valley deeps,
as the healing sun
seals the haemophiliac flow.

The valley blooms
to new poems
written on olive skins,
the empty space to giant pizzas
from Ponzanelli's,
the thirsty rock to cocktails
brewed and shaken
to Valentino's recipe.
How the smell of frangipani
gently surrenders
to Jergens Lotion, Lilac Spray
and brandy on the rocks.

How the small linear star
melts to the fluid circle
of the sun,
and her gilded voice leaps
from the cougar's throat.
How the moon spills
her lotus eyes,
and white rock sprouts
with raven hair;
How the blue water at Fergus Dam
thrashes the soft brown skin
and sun face.
A slim Singhala girl
stretches in his bones
across the wide open world,

the vine hangs heavy again
with purple grape.

FT

Kamala

Kamala, my love,
let's not search
for the blood on the north star,
or the wound of fingers
that dragged the talapath and seer
from this adolescent sea.

Let's not probe the grass
for the polished head
of the cobra,
or count the pink coconuts
strewn with the knife of beetle
in their throats.

Let's not think of nights
when the firefly refused to burn,
or how the monsoon rain
grew leopard's jaws
on the blue face of the sea.

True,
home hangs on the fin of a fish
and my life would cling on
to your flat feet
and bare breasts
as you move from corner to corner
dispensing destinies
of hot tea and fried fish.

What if our children
born with the cinnabar of sea
under their tongues, anemones
in their eyes,
spend their waking hours
where the turtle hides its eggs,
come home only to unravel
their seaweed dreams

under a thatch of leaves?

Disregard
the tales of travellers
that break through our fishnet lives:
how amber jewels
catch fire in Ratnapura's bosom,
or how elephants walk
under a Panamure moon
with ivory big as catamarans.

They wouldn't speak
of cardboard shacks
crumbling in the rain,
or the decaying breath
of Pettah's alleys,
or how sunburnt beggars
limp with pariah dogs
in search of the breath of rice.

Let's sit here, my love,
by the edge of the sea
and read the horoscopes
of our fishing lives:
how very like the turbulence
of the sea's rabana heart,
and yet
the gentle rise and fall
of its soft blue ribs.

And somewhere
on our cow-dung floor,
don't we have a coral palace
of sun-fish bones,
shell dishes of crab
and seaweed to bind
our burning limbs.

And when the sun
has blushed itself to sleep
on the curved lap of the horizon,
let's go home
to the rice pot on the fire,
coconut toddy
and the smell of seer and salt
from the ever-giving sea.

Kamala, my love,
we are the spawn of the sea,
and home is here
under these cracked rafters
and pale thatch of leaves.
Beyond
        lies a strange land
where we can only wear
a face of alien skin,
and not finding
the fin of fish or salt of sea
we'll slowly die within ourselves.

NOTE: A found poem. From a conversation between an old fisherman
and his wife on a beach in Ceylon.

FT

talapath and seer: varieties of fish
Ratnapura: a town in Sri Lanka known for its precious stones
Panamure: a small town in north central Sri Lanka
Pettah: commercial district in Colombo
rabana: a Sri Lankan drum, often used during the sinhala new-year
festivities
coconut toddy: popular alcoholic drink

Love Poem

For Anne

For you, brown lover,
with buffalo curd and palmyrah honey
still sweet on your lips,
the raven winging in your hair,

I offer the immigrant land
with no contrary season,
only summer,
and summer and summer.

No white laming cold before the thaw,
no cutting nodule of spring,
no fallen leaves to confuse your feet,
only the consummate thing,

the full-blown rose, the sun
in batik exuberance.

Now also ask for the sweet warm rain,
the once monsoon harvest of fruit:
jambu, mango and mangosteen;
guava and rambuttan, the tender cadju

wrapped in green leaves, the jaggery bell
of the godambara-roti man,
and I will tease the Asian condiment
from the summer almirahs of this land.

What you deserve will be
what you always had
in your warm rich blood:

the green land.

SW

19

palmyrah: a palm tree
batik: multicoloured fabric
mangosteen: an applelike fruit, purple in colour
rambuttan: a small fruit with fleshy interior
godambara roti: a pancake made out of flour
almirah: portuguese for cupboard

Love Poem for Anne #4

Never one to utter easily
the gaga word, or fall clumsily
into a warm hug,
other passionate gestures
seeming always so heavy and unbecoming
as cheap perfume.

No kissing spasms, here,
no bear hugs,
or other strange use
of the body's exotic language;
just a sniff (the a la Ceylon kiss)
on your broad forehead,
or sweet brown cheeks;
sometimes, your raven head.

My long deep silences.
The torment
of that lonely white beach   for me,
(for you) where I waited long
for the Muse
who never came. . .

You moved in and out
of my dark moods like a saint,
keeping to your homely chores,
knowing

I was always there—
a nylon sea holding a love poem
beneath its calm white skin.

We both knew
of the faking colours of love,
of honey that once dripped
from the soft mouths of courting men,
women with cosmetic faces,
exaggerated gestures   words:
"I love you, honey, I will always love you"

And then the hard mouths, fists,
beautiful corpses
under the evergreens, the distant elms;
the *order nisi,* baby in a dumpster,
a hungry hit man prowling
like a shadow seeking out
a cold scheming wife.

For two months now, you
have found you sweet cinnabar
of Sri Lankan sun;
Now let the healing lasers
soothe your arthritic bones;
go for the card games, the milk wine,

halapay, dhodol, and rice cakes;
suck the sweet dampera,
then ask for the guava and the jak
that ripens like gold in your sister's backyard;
tell the raven and the elephant
I still sing their extravagant song,
parade their metaphors
without compromise.

I see three loving sisters,
lazy, like beached mermaids, on the old bed,
licking up the year's gossip:

how aunty Maud broke her hip
trying to tie her shoe laces,
the postman that ran away with
the hamu-mahathmaya's wife.

I won't mention
Colombo's walking dead,
the suicide bombers, the blood
that flows so freely in the dusty North.
Be calm; death is no greater lover than life,
each will seed and explode
in its own season.

I miss you.   I, who couldn't find
the words to say I love you
when you were here, warm by my side,
now resort to this poor surrogate
of a poem. Yes   I miss you
as I miss the sun
and rain of my green days,

not the sweet mechanic
of household machinery,
nor the woman who makes magic
on the hot stove.
But, your presence   those spaces
of your walking, the unspoken love,
this absence, this silence,   this night without firefly
that's now mine
can only seek refuge

in the arms of the Muse.

New

milk wine: a sweet wine popular among Burghers
halapay: sweet made out of flour
dhodol: sweet made out of flour and milk
dampera: a small sweet mango
hamu-mahathmaya: a person of influence and standing

The Marshmallow Land

From Shovel to Self-propelled Blower:
The Immigrant's Progress

Two days into the Promised Land
and my eyes dance:
supermarket and mall,
those shopping faces thick with neon,
plastic cards breathing under their breasts.
One block, and the GOLDEN OX rises
with MOLSON froth and snaking smoke,
afternoon men angular in beer laughter.
I am in TV's arms.
I laugh with the HONEYMOONERS,
the Cuban and his Lucy,
trace blood along the FUGITIVE's trail.
No one mentioned the forecast: tomorrow
100% precipitation / freezing rain.
So down the shimmering street I go
with only my sun head and ADIDAS,
to learn how the feet suddenly slide,
shudder with instant pain,
the body lumps to horizontal woe.
3 broken ribs, some hefty pain,
I've learnt the beatitudes of ice,
something sacred, something cold,
demanding respect, a paraphernalia
of horned boots, cowl and padded vest,
for body nicely flexed to winter's mould.

After twenty winters in my bones,
shovelling my sidewalk snow,
a self-propelled blower called Pablo
now does my chores,
                    vertical as my front door,

and I'm happy.

SR

After the Snowfall

Through garage door lookouts,
winter hazed:

bleached bones   the catalpa
(without   its green crinoline head)

king maple   so humbled
frail white arms   skying

a tree
praying for its life

driveway   divided
snow walls   on either side

the Red Sea   parted again
and Moses   nowhere in sight

But Pharaoh   on his snowplough
continues history: walls the last exit,

laughs: there shall be no diaspora today!

O Lord, mine are summer eyes—
tomorrow   the promised land?

your Egypt   shill shimmers and shines
in its white   misery

BI

Civilization

Dollar-Daze, Days
at Zellers County Fair,
and the parking lot
like some African watering hole,
gathers in its animals.

The way they spill out
of their polished automobile skins,
drooling with Dollar-Daze,
ham on rye, the second cup free.

Supermarket vertigo,
and like everybody else
I roam the gleaming jungle,
now nowhere near the centre (of reason)
nothing but my head full

of cut prices, secret desires
to squeeze the CHARMIN,
jaws tight
on the raw meat of civilization.

Soon, I'm no more the hunter
but the hunted
as shelves beckon, seduce
like women of the evening,

and I surrender
to HEAVENLY HASH, pig tails,
cocktail wieners, almost anything
that bears a price slash on its face.

O God, I now feel
like the plastic bauble
at two-for-a-dollar,
the 50% discount coat
hanging limp and old

on its rack,

am surging
with the hysterical women
for the shimmering polyester satin,
the Velours warm as blood,
watching how their eyes burn
like warring gods,
becoming
just another shape
on a sewing machine.

All this metaphor
for nothing
but food, clothing and shelter?

RD

The Interview

Two TV cameras trained like guns,
I, the sun-man,
your caressing eyes,
and the countdown . . .

You coax me into beginnings,
past inventions in the snow,
then deftly persuade deeper fires,
my thin Canadian ice
to thaw in my throat,
the maple lead smudge in my passport.

I am in the mouth of the sun,
the Immigrant's Song,
how I hear the elephant in my sleep;
white landscape in ruins,

I find my own, green forest, island sea:
the ocelot's eye, the jambu bleeds,
my childhood dream
in the claws of the sand crab.

And what shaped your book
Flesh and Thorn?
Blood on the sun,
the Scarlet Ibis blurred in the Swamp,
how deceit crouched in the crotch,
"love, with his gift of pain."

Suddenly, I split the act in two,
juggle two red balls,
the poem made, the poem becoming:
I swim in your saucer eyes,
fingers search the curved fruit
under your shirt,
I nose ebony configurations,
dream the almond under the husk . . .

EI

For the Winter Man

For you
I bring gifts
of myrrh and cassia,
white ivory
heavy as boulders,
sweet blood of jambu.

I have truths
the colour of bougainvillaea,
parables plucked from sunsets,

29

eternal
as the core of the Buddha.

But winter's myths
have reached deep
into the marrow,
and there is now
no other way to the summer sun
but through a thick vein of ice.

Nothing will shake the discipline
of your season's clock,
melt the blue rinks of your eyes.
Like a puck
you'll remain silent hammered
into a corner
in winter's measured arena.

But when summer comes,
and the geometries of our moods
touch like tangents,
you'll no doubt accept these gifts
from the sun-man.

Until then,
aren't we all
the fossils of our seasons?
You, horizontal in your deep sleep of ice,
I,
vertical
in the shadows
of the sun,
dancing
like a clown
with fire
on my feet.

EI

After the K-W Writer's Award

The eulogium,
nothing but meat and gravy!

My prize statue catches fire
under the arc lights,

is heavy as brass,
weighs me down like an anchor

as I stagger back
to my front-row seat.

How fame hints at humbling ballasts,
stones at the core.

Why now, Rilke, your voice against victory,
that "to endure is all"?

How this woman sidles up
and asks: "Where are you from?"
Soft baby blues (mask green,
hate, as in hooded clansman)

search for fault lines
in my skin, black eyes.

Sorry, lady, I have nothing
but the sweetness of silence,

I've already done
with my fire and my song.

BI

He who rides the elephant
Remains undisturbed
By the barking dogs   KABIR

They swagger out of China Town's
Kung-fu Hotel,

two skinheads, Aryan blue eyes,
mouths already flavoured with Chinese fried rice,

egg rolls, tiger prawns in bean sauce,
and hate.

The fortune cookie read: 'Today, you'll meet
the sun-man, sinner and saint'

"OK. Let's haze this po-faced podge !
Paki, Paki, which fucking sky did you fall from?"

Stone. Silence. Elephant. Saint.
My black belt stirs, coils back to sleep.

Barely into a rosary
of forgiving thoughts,

when the skunk words
dissolve into the soured air like a smoke.

New

Elegy for the Sun-man's Children Going

For Daphne, Maria, John

How he plunged bravely
from sun to snow,
made the perfect metaphor
from elephant and ice,
the breath of his sun children,
but never stepped out of the womb.

Time ran his fingers
thro their spring-rained hair,
saw their small bodies burgeon
like new grass, fashion words
from the puberty of a season;

And June broke cottage carnival,
their sun
spun headily on a frisbee,
love on the shuttlecock's nose,
the barbecue ripening like summer fruit.

And he shared their days
of shedding leaves,
winter's cruel gaucherie,
a stylish log fire
in his rice, and curry, and heart.

But the road that forked
like a divided vein,
took in its restless travellers:
and Daphne was gone, Maria is going,
and John contemplates the cobalt sky
with adolescent eyes, the possible mileage
in his sneakers.

This immigrant poet,
whose road was never his, but went,

taking them to the junction
of their dreams, a pilgrim
without pilgrimage, his altar
still like the warm smooth stone
that stayed in the sun.

EI

Interpreting the Clothesline

The fat lady sings
   as she steps into her backyard:
student guests
   sweat and swarm
over their smoking barbeque.

Over the fence,
   the coloured minutiae
of another civilization?
   The neighbour's clothesline
fluttering alien flags.
But where there's Molson, porkchops,
   sausages and the girls
from Village 1
   cultural anthropology, sociology of dress
have no place on the menu.

Not so for the fat lady.
   She's into social inquiry,
gossip. "Getting to know
   your immigrant neighbour!"
So, what if she dares to catalogue,
   interpret those dancing items
that she's never seen
   or known before?

A dashiki simmers in gold and green;
     two sarongs stew
in their exotic dyes; black Gandhi jacket,
gold-laced saris, bedsheets
     with pink elephants walking all over them;
baby sleepers that parade sand crabs
     in a praying mode; an Arya-Singhala suit
taking in the afternoon sun.

Dashiki: a large loose-fitting buttonless shirt.
     Fat lady: "Must be what hula-hula man wears!"
Sarong: a draped skirtlike garment
     worn by men and women in the Malayan Archipelago,
Sri Lanka and the Pacific Islands.
     Fat lady: "What the hell is that?
Seamless piece of cloth like a tube with show flowers
     blooming all over it like crazy."

Sari: outer garment, long piece of cloth
     wrapped around the body
with one end over the head.
     Fat lady: "My! What soft material!
What do they use it for?
     To cover themselves,
or bury their dead?"

The fat lady shakes her head.
     Her beady eyes
still frozen on her neighbour's laundry line
     like an Irish setter's.
"Who are these people?" she asks herself,
     pinching her pink thighs
in utter frustration.

"Do elephants, sand crabs, strange flowers,
     gross and glaring colours
crowd their lives
     as do their clothes?
Must be some alien farmer type

with no notion whatever
of fashion, style or decor!"

"Who knows. Could be even
    Asian gypsies or carnival circus folks!"

New

Remains of an Asian Poet Writing in Canada

About the butterfly
that flapped
amber
in the cerebral land

How winter
was made equal
to summer
and the skin glowed
like an oiled Brahmin
and bangles grew
on naked trees

And summer
blew orioles
salad of mango
and the bird of paradise
draped its wings
on the concrete land

They found
saffron wings
raw
on a smooth stone

The skull
separate   still green
in the dark wound
of a tree

A thigh
bronze warm
with the maul
of thorns

And they found
the sun dead
under the snow

EI

Hypotheticals

If I bleach
my brown skin,

fashion the crow eyes
to lapis lazuli,

let the blonde magic
run through my wild black hair;

If I exchange
my halting lilt

for a measured accent,
the maple rooted under my tongue,
damn the rustic arrack
for all its fire,
and sip the dry highball
with black-tie elegance;

If I give up my elephant amble
for an athletic stride,

forsake the curry, the tempered rice,
for meat and potatoes,

dream my nightly batik song
in silk pyjamas.

Will these translations hold?
These erasures stay clean and credible?

Would I then
shimmer before your eyes

Like the Lake's skin
at high noon?

New

Sitting Alone in the Happy Hour Cafe

and meeting civilization head on
with a doughnut, hot coffee, a cigarette.
At the centre table,
suddenly thinking of horseshoes.
What if somebody mistakes me
for a target,
begins to practice his Western art?
Cigarette smoke snakes above my head,
makes a highway,
collapses.

I'm being watched.
Blue eyes suddenly a torment,
a torrent of waterfall,

beauty with a knife between its teeth.
So once again, I must close my black eyes,
feel my legs climbing,
climbing
towards the sun.
Each crag, jutting root,
now a rung of mercy.

I must move, move
away from this darkness unasked for,
or make that second discovery
of fire: love
for the tall man with thrusting blue eyes
seeing nothing
but a blur of shadowed skin
a spot on his morning sun.

SR

The Unhyphenated Canadians

Who are these men
with faces
the colour of night,
their heads, their hair, their eyes,   black,
who talk in strange tongues?

Who are these men
whose bravado is of the sun,
who walk in dark clothes
at high noon,
clutter these streets
like shadows?

Whose snow
seems to melt

under the fire of their feet,
and for whom freezing rain
is nothing but a monsoon shower;
Does the skirling wind
mask their effusive voices
like a long, slow moan?

The Johnnny Walker's Club.
I encounter one fellow
nursing a martini,
another with his favourite Blue, most
with arrack fire
churning in their bellies.

They are the unhyphenated Canadians
who talk poetry and politics
as if they just stepped out
of the Learneds;
mention deficits,
and they'll spin numbers
round your head
like a web.

Some of them bank executives
after crunching numbers
the whole day long
help out at the Metro Soup Kitchen,
dark men   at home
among the homeless,
their white aprons
like fireflies on a tar night.

They don't talk,
rave or rant about the stabbing moments.
No words or gestures suggest
the odd darkness, the civilized assassin
that stalks their lives,
only the sea-calm in their charcoal eyes,
karma and a lone raven   riding
their rocking souls.   *New*

40

Dark Antonyms and Paradise

Roots

For Cleta Marcellina Nora Serpanchy

What the end usually demands
is something of the beginning,
and so
I conjure history from a cup
of warm Portuguese blood
from my forefathers,
black diamond eyes, charcoal hair
from my Sinhalese mothers;
the beached catamaran,
gravel voices of the fishermen,
the catch still beating like a heart
under the pelting sun;
how the pariah dogs looked urgent
with fish meal in their brains,
the children romped, sagged,
then melted into the sand.

A Portuguese captain holds
the soft brown hand of my Sinhala mother.
It's the year 1515 AD,
when two civilizations kissed and merged,
and I, burgher of that hot embrace,
write a poem of history
as if it were only the romance
of a lonely soldier on a crowded beach
in southern Ceylon.

SW

Bouquet to My Colonial Masters

Gauguin's woman under another sun
raped. How silence spilled
from an abattoir of tongues.

And you still show me
your polished bannisters,
your country estates,
green, columned and groomed.

How your freighters coughed black,
then guffawed and left heavy
with coconut and tea,
cardamom, cinnamon and ivory,
the sandalwood artifacts
still leaking their exotic perfume
from their dark holds.

And through it all
I heard the Englishman's siesta snore,
the civilized cooing
of civilized men
gulping their velvet whiskies,
as brown waiters bent and bowed
to the evening noise of their masters.

So what was left to keep?
Shakespeare!
a tongue to speak with,
some words to remember.
Today,
we are all poets
for having suffered the chains,
for having learnt the language.

RD

The Word Made Good

High noon.
The Plantation sags,   sweats
under Haputale's mauling sun.
The bloodsucker on the lawn
is pure sculpture, the rosebud
a phantasmagoria of blood.

In the Superintendent's bungalow,
siesta holds the Englishman stiff
on his divan, his eyes folded.
The veranda barely hides the servants
drooping
like flowers in a vase.

Not for long—
the master's voice booms
at a bare-bodied man
standing arrogant
at the door, his rifle
catching the afternoon sun
through the window like a mirror.

"Who are you?
What the hell do you want?"
"I am Sardiel of Uttuwankande.
I want 131 rupees immediately,
not a cent more or less.
Will you lend me the money, Sir?"
"Yes, but why this exact amount,
and why demand such a paltry sum
at the point of a gun?"

"Today, as the half-moon
crawls over the Rock,
I need to pay my debt to Carolis,
a poor villager. Monies borrowed
(also at the point of a gun)

for my gambling at cards.
Sardiel of Uttuwankande
always keeps his word."

He is last seen
on his knees   bending over
to smell the roses.

Stunned servants crowd the divan,
the head appu protesting:
     "Master doing foolish thing.
     Big rogue this Sardiel,
     very dangerous man, too.
     Master should call police."

"No. Have you heard the name 'Robin Hood'?"

Bungalow gossip
hardly two days old,
when a hulking man stands at the front door,
hands the houseboy a large package.
Rolled in leopard's skin
is the Englishman's rifle,
the servant's sword,
and a crocodile skin
bulging with 131 rupees!

BI

Haputale: a city in the hill country of Sri Lanka
veranda: an open porch along the outside of a house
appu: butler or head servant

You Cannot Tell Me That I'm Not an Elephant

You cannot tell me
that I'm not an elephant

because I stood apart from the herd,
spilled my elegy in whispers
and trumpeted the last post for a dying bull;
the magic of my memory,
how I trampled my mahout to death
for a ten-year-old harassing word, unkind prod.

Because I often lie on my back
with my thick legs vertical
to the Serengeti stars;
make music (instead of
the hyena's murderous bark)
whenever I call to the sensuous moon
as it rides over the Acacia tree.

Because I can blow smoke
through my trunk,
play the mouth organ,
swivel on a wooden stool
two feet in diameter,
pick a pin from a haystack
with the magnet of my nose.

You cannot tell me
that I'm not an elephant.

Because I am wise
in the ways of water,
smell a waterhole miles across the plains,
can dig a life-saving well with my bare tusks;
because I sleep standing
without ever rolling over,
with only my big ears flapping
in the night breeze.

Because it seems odd to you
that my great bulk
can ride on leaf and woodapple,
the sweet bark that fights desperately
to stay with its tree like a body suit;
because I can talk to my family
twenty miles away
with a voice beyond and below the human ear.

You cannot tell me
that I'm not an elephant.

Because I know the pain
in the sound of the chains,
the harassing voice dream
of green Africa, the virgin forests,
the waterhole that once gathered the great herds
as if for a common baptism.

Because I know
the time of my going
(when the bicuspids in my mouth
have sunk beneath my gums
and I can no longer chew the sweet bark
or stem of leaf)
and my old legs take me as in dream
to the graveyard of my brothers.

Dark Antonyms in Paradise

O my beloved country,
I return like the prodigal,
stay for sixty days
and sixty nights; return,
to warm my arthritic bones,
listen to your heartbeat,
your new song, what media

and the London *Economist* declared
was the new redemption, the prosperity
Hongkong and Singapore style.
How JR, like the great Dutugemunu
builds another brazen palace
by the marshes of Kotte,
and now rests in his silken sarong
and ripened dreams.

Two million rupees
flow daily like milk and honey
to your desert bowls, your people's
sweat in Dubai and Oman,
the sweet sands of Arabia;
and a hundred thousand now eat cake,
where once they couldn't find
a fistful of rice.

And a man from Attanagala
ends his life
with a gulp of Ecotax.
And so did his wife and two daughters
two months earlier. The coroner
regretted the lack of early
psychiatric treatment.

I've seen the bustle and buzz
of your Free Trade Zone,
the new adventures, American banks,

Japanese technology,
how hundreds of village girls
with money on their morning faces
move briskly to man the spindles, the levers
that make their new-found bread.

And a seventy-year-old man,
distressed over his prolonged illness
from snake bite,
throws himself body and soul
before the Galle Evening Express.

And how your Galle Road highway throbs
to the low hum of the Mercedes,
a thousand Toyota bodies moving
like a cluster of dragonflies in the sun;
and the trishaws, Izuki buses
in which your brown bodies ride
with the disciplined patience of ants.

And a twelve-year-old student
embraces his sweet grave
with a generous potion of Paraquat
because his mother chided him
for quarrelling with his sister.

Five-star hotels now gleam
in the Sri Lanka sun, tourists
dip their bottoms
in the everlasting blue
of your circling sea, wrap
their pink skins in cotton and silks,
the loud embrace of batik;
and your craft boutiques burst
at their seams with elephant and ivory,
the filigree effusions
of your artistic people.

And another twelve-year-old
chooses an untimely grave
with Endrex,
because his teacher caned him
for forgetting his drawing book.

O my beloved country,
your paradise story goes on and on
with dark antonyms to match.
But take a bow, an encore,
and an encore for the warm brilliance
of your new sun.
I pray
for slum corners of your kingdom,
your soul.

SW

JR.: J R Jayawardene, former president of Sri Lanka
Dutugemunu: a king of Ceylon celebrated as a national hero
Kotte: ancient city in Sri Lanka
Attanagala: a village in central Sri Lanka

In the Shadow of the Tiger (1)

Postcard: Colombo, 25 July, 1987

Fawzi & Co took me to the Liberty Plaza
not before the Security searched our car
and ran us down with some electronic rod.
I giggled when the searching rod
slid down my pelvic area;
safe inside—half the folks, however,
seemed to me like Tamil Tigers who had
escaped the net. I was convinced otherwise
only when I heard their Singhala Only accents
and saw the way they gobbled the pattis
at the corner stall.
New Zealand and Australian cheeses are here!
Throw in some fresh fish like talapath
the blood still dripping from their fins.
Came home loaded with groceries, including
Johnny Walker and two bottles of Mendis Special Arrack.
Poorer by 4000 bucks.

love you

R

PS—I overheard this guy telling his girl friend
that 10 Tigers captured in Batticaloa
ended their dream with the cyanide capsules
carried round their necks.

ciao rienzi

SR

Tigers: a Tamil militant group

Galle Road (Sri Lanka)
or: The Tango of Flesh and Fender

Galle Road: the gorged python highway
from Colombo to the deep south.
If you must drive,
wishing to live,
listen to these guidelines:

Leave your nerves at home.
Put on the thin armour of brinkmanship,
art that moves your fender
within an inch of pedestrian flesh,
that grazes the Toyota bodies
so that you can smell their new paint.
You move steadily forward,
inch by inch, hanging on their tails.
You scratch not, you spill no blood.

Understand clearly
the Island's philosophy
of man and machine:
no traffic lights command,
flesh and bone set the pace,
give directions. An old man
stumbling in infirmity
across the highway
stops a two-ton truck dead in its tracks.

Children, old women,
beggars, working girls, rice hounds
command the flow, the stop and go,
can move across, in between,
wherever their bodies and spirits
take them.
You can spit and curse and chase,
You touch not, you spill no blood.

Use your horn profusely.
Here, the hot and humid air
lulls the reflexes to dream.
We recommend a Kawasaki horn,
the model whose decibel pitch
is guaranteed
to pry drowsing eyelids.

Remember always
the components of your highway:
people: moving restless people of the sun;
and weaving cyclists, trishaws,
bullock cars, hand carts, pingo men,
huge Izuki buses, pariah dogs, cattle (closer
to the south)
and the sunstroked precision
of a thousand mad drivers.

Watch out especially
for the Trishaw men
bobbing and weaving
through highway space like acrobats,
their hearts and yours
full in the mouth.

If you need to stop
along the way,
do not coast gently to your spot.
Signal, then stop with fire
in your brakes.
The other driver, a half inch behind,
will wake up for his life.

Finally, we repeat:
Understand the sequence of locomotion, here:
first man, then machine.
The highway python will move slowly
but surely forward,
no twisted fender, no smell of blood.

Here, the world's greatest urban drivers
display the art supreme of brinkmanship:
How under a hammering sun,
they dance the tango
of flesh and fender
without each ever touching the other.

SW

Ritual at Dawn

For the children of the village of Boralesgamuva, Sri Lanka

A thin yellow light seeps through
the banana leaves; jak fruit and coconut,
the trumpet mouth of the shoe flower
are caught in the halo of the sun.
The croton hedge wears a veil of fire.
All doors and windows are flung open
to the returning world.

Like a fervent morning prayer
a child sweeps the front yard
with an eekle broom, shores
the dog shit and dead leaves to a corner,
smoothes the red pebbles, sand,
to look like dawn's Indian Sea.
The garbage fire will soon end
the story of night's intruders.

As the bamboo gate shakes
to the irreverent crows,
a mynah bird settles quietly for breakfast.
And the children
grow their dreams in the sand
playing their thin voices, their morning bones,

jumping the hopscotch bases
with the muscle and laughter
of a new day.

Only a blaring radio of Singhala love songs
violate these burgeoning hours.

SW

Boralesgamuva: a village outside Colombo
eekle broom: a broom made from the spine of the coconut leaf

Rice

Michael,
it's time to let go:
mother's milk, those other founts
that spread like water
at your roots.
But don't talk of pablum
or ask for Heinz or Gerber's,

ask for ceremonies
of rice soft boiled,
Lanka's first and solid sequel
to mother's milk.

When you enter the heart
of the paddies, you enter
the mouths of your fathers,
a nation, continents,
half the world (living and breathing
in a grain of rice)

And you'll grow strong
and straight as a coconut tree.
Look at you,

how the paddies
have fulfilled their promise;
how you love the taste of basmati,
the samba grains, distinct and separate
as pearls.

But now,
up here in snow land,
you have turned against rice,
embraced the wiener between the bun,
some dog called "hot,"
a mouthful of yellow chips,
salted, serrated, barbecued;

I watch the fries disappear
in your mouth like quicksand;
your daily ritual
of hamburgers (with everything on it)
spread their juice down your shirt,
your new-found throat.

Son,
somewhere in the paddy lands,
a farmer still gives his bare back
to the cruel sun,
the buffalo, their thick wearied legs
to the plough,
and the mud furrows will again
sprout the paddies

to feed a world
that you know no more.

BI

basmati and samba: varieties of rice

He Who Talks to the Raven

talks to God,
    black feathered and beaked
with toe nails growing inward,
    a mouth full of caw;
superb surveyor of the skies,
    postman to history
happening by the second,
    foul mouthed, he sings
the sweetest song, black eyed
    he outdoes the morning sun.

He who talks to the raven
    shares parables,
some windows of possibility:
    if the water's at the bottom
of the pitcher,
    throws pebble after pebble
and the level will rise like bread
    to the top.
If the desert churns its thirst
    knows that there's water
breeding in the cactus.

He who talks to the raven
    talks to the bird humming
with ESP in its brain:
    who knows the distant agony
of the goat even as the anaconda
    unhinges its jaws;
the byways of the eagle's ether flight
    before it traps
the rabbit's frozen eyes.

He who talks to the raven
    long enough, learns
how the sweet wood apple
    disappears in the elephant's mouth,

how to say: caw   caw   caw
      when the gongs of hunger
ring like church bells.
      How when something lurches,
is ready to strike,
      can suddenly stride
into the face of the sun,
      keep the rose between his teeth
and say: caw   caw   caw.

This bird is bore
      and diplomat,
will take your gifts
      and demand for more, insist
that your understand its importunate ways,
      love it, stroke its velvet wing.

When the raven talks,
      listen,
it is God
      in ultimate disguise.

RD

Memory's Truth

I've left the green land,

          mother country—
So what thoughts
        will ever silence

the infant footfalls
      on red cement floors,
restore the omphalos blood
         that sang my green days?

How argue the diaspora?

       Would I let nostalgia
flirt with hyperbole?
      Is there enough love
to conjure past perfections,
         forget, forgive
those strident voices
    the arrythmia of the wicked heart?

I know. I'll make the coconut tree
      forever straight,
without hint of midnight beetle   deep
   in the pink fruit's throat.

There's a raging moon,
        the fruit bat's nightly orgy is on,
but cadju-pulang and mango
       will still be whole and sweet
as newborn toddy—
   nothing will fester
under this extravagant sun,
        the fruit fly will not feast.

As for the monsoon rain,
       there'll only be the beautiful slant

of raindrops,
        cool massage,
me dancing naked
        under God's own shower head;
and the havocking floods,
        mud huts dissolving like chocolate?
bloated bodies
        riding the dark currents to the sea?

I wouldn't know.

From here,
        this imperfect beautiful land,
new entrances seem
        rational, imperative;
old exits survive, ride
        the sweet inventions of memory;
the green land
        forever green,
the lost country
        ever perfect.

BI

The Igloo of Heaven

Immigrant

At forty,
the bone had set,
           hard as stone;
the belly conditioned
to rice, curry, and strong tea.
My love for Anne
and my hatred for John
basked naked
           like stone pillars
in my courtyard.
Lesser likes and dislikes
grew wild as weeds,
and I could pluck them out at will
with my bare hands,
here, where there was no metaphor
but the sun.

Now I hear
the wild geese squawk their throats in flight
at the promise of white ruin,
the snow that covered all:
my Anne, my John, my lilies, my weeds.
How a film of ice spun round my skin,
fires that sputtered to a white wind
and died with a curse on their jaws.

But somehow,
I remember the roots
of my crow hair,
Anne and John struggling in their shadows,
wild lilies and weeds
                 straining
their thin bones
                 against a crust of ice,
waiting
   to break loose.

For the time being, perhaps,
no one will know my real name
or guess where I really come from.
Who'll ever know
that I was once mad
in the carnival of the sun,
when I now live
              without
my loves and hates,
wild lilies or weeds,
only the passion
              of the unsaid word,
the white silence
              of civilization.

EI

Faces of the Sun-man

Descendent
        of the sun,
he comes with the colour of skin
in bronze,
a bone distilled
in the Vedic poem,
a psalm of peace
locked in his Buddha eyes.

He is a body
of blue water
shaped like a man,
limpid to the depths;
you can look or move
into him, through him,
the fluid dimension holds.

Sticks and stones
only ripple his face
like a tentative breeze,
and sink
to cool their fires.

When silence threatens,
he cries for the shake
of the sun's thunder,
splinters glass
with the wild trumpet
of elephant, coaxes
a leopard's growl
from the muscles of his belly.

When noise strikes,
he walks, like an octopus,
into his limbs,
plugs his small brown ears
with sun-stained olives,
and waits
for the decibels
to climb down to the pitch
of the magpie's song.

When hate wears
a white mud mask,
and dances in rituals
of living death,
he holds out a golden hand
marinated in the sun,
a Jesus heart plucked
from some ancient Calvary.

When winter comes,
he crawls
into his sundial nerves
and sleeps
with myths and shibboleths,

as central heating steals
under his dark eyelids,

to dream of blue Ceylon,
where palms bend
their coconut breasts
to the morning sun,
and Nuwera-Eliya's valley
oozes with the fragrance of tea,
the sunstroked fishermen swearing
under their salty breath
as they clown
with the rush of toddy
in their black skulls.

When spring breaks,
he hears the paddy bird's song
in his throat, watches
the kingfisher bend its wing
to the blue lotus, the sun
trap the dagoba spires
with rings of fire.

He's sipped the ferment
of Red Cap Ale,
jumped to the slithering puck
on Saturday Night Hockey,
smelled Ali Baba's steaks
grow rich on slow charcoal fires,
but loves to grab the batik spice
of rice and curry,
to beat his thighs with green leaves,
write poems
the colour of wounded sunsets.

When his neighbour's lawn
shines with the summer shave
of mower and prong,
he turns green

and steals, a mantis
in the long grass,
to sleep
with a symphony
of dandelion and weed
about his green ears.

He is the son
   of the sun,
   shaped like fire,
   bound in cap and bells,
   a dusky clown
   beating winter's silence
   to a bellyful of laughter.

EI

Vedic: pertaining to the Hindu scriptures
Nuwara-Eliya: a city in the hill country, popular among tourists

In the Idiom of the Sun

It would have been somewhat different
in green Sri Lanka, where I touched
the sun's fire daily
with my warm finger tips.

I wouldn't have hesitated
to call you a bastard
and for emphasis, might have even
thrown in the four-letter word.

The blood would have shuddered a little
under your Aryan skull,
but you would have held my honesty
like a Temple flower in full bloom,
forgiven my holy idiom.

Here in this white land,
the senses forged to iron silence,
the mind trapped in a snow boot,
I must hold my black tongue.

The blood has wintered,
and icicles hang like cobwebs
from the roof of my cold mouth.
I can now only spit frozen eyed,
and gently demur.

SW

Song of the Immigrant

It's time
to break your elephant and wood-apple dream.
Honey and curd in your mouth,
the kingfisher ablaze by the Mahaveli's edge—
time to cast off
your batik sarong, wooden thongs,
the exotic shackles round your throat.

You only read
the language of signs,
a long silence in the snow,
a dark music   silent
and hammered in your blood.

No more shall the elders say:
Hold your tongue and wait,
this night will pass.
The civilized nerves
will first grow taut, then break;
then sleep beside your alien breath,
then love you with a tentative smile,

even bleed for your leftover pain.
Now you may talk loudly of crows
as stars in a dark night,
conjure peacocks from harvest cornfields,
look straight into the sun, the whipping snow
and not blink at all.
Be happy now.
Only death
can redeem
the original dream.

SR

Mahaveli: the longest river in Sri Lanka

Why I Can Talk of the Angelic Qualities of the Raven

Let's talk colours.
Start with BLACK,
that true hallmark of the sun.
What else
is the eye of the hurricane, the colour
of magic night?
Is the Geisha, Geisha
without her black crown
against porcelain skin?
If the raven talks, listen.
It's God in winged disguise.

What's coloured
(blue, cinnabar, turquoise)
always throbs like a lover's heart.
The bougainvillaea
under a Trinidad sun
holds the magic of metaphors,
sets off the quality

of our sunsets, our batik effusions,
our Gauguins, our murders.

As for WHITE
read the instructions carefully:
FRAGILE HANDLE WITH CARE THIS SIDE UP
May be too precious
for ordinary use, extraordinary pain;
the angelic colour
often overwhelms,
is much like strobe glare
over desert sands.

And what about BROWN
or its variants:
olive, beige, sunburnt yellow?

they hardly preach, intrude,
refuse to wilt under the sun
and yet, could be
as lush and vibrant
as a Kandyan maid.

No; colour has nothing to do with it.
What you imagine
is all that matters.
The rest is too real to be true.
The apple was only cinema,
so was the serpent, the woman.
What was real
was Original Sin.
Adam slapping God
on his cosmic ears.

RD

Kandyan: a person from Kandy, the hill capital of Sri Lanka

Still Close to the Raven

After twenty winters in their bones
summers red as immortelle
trees that danced wildly naked
for twenty falls

he would say
raven
the old cabook house
sandcrab
the Buddha
with his Vesak face
snow
ice creamed on the lawn
fireside embers
sherry in one hand
"I've tasted my blood"
in the other

And she
the pingo man
his rambuttans
sweet as jaggery
the long sun
like gravy in my mouth
the fishmonger's cry
children   loud
and angular at the Cricket Match
the Godambara roti man
his bell and smoking oil lamp
gently closing
the eyelids of the sun

SR

Vesak: the day the Buddha attained enlightenment

The Rain Doesn't Know Me Any More

I, who for so long
shaped the forgotten metaphor:
curved tusks, howdah
and mahout of elephant.
Who splashed the Bird of Paradise
against a cemetery of cars,
sought the root in cabook earth,
the dream   that meandered, got lost
in an orgasm of blood.
I, who held the palm tree's silhouette
against the going sun, a woman,
a child   long enough
to divide a continent,
have new revelations:
I have circled the sun.
The white marshmallow land is now mine,
conquered, cussed upon,
loved.

Look at this other dreaming face,
these new muscles, tempered bones,
black eyes, blue
with a new landscape, legs
dancing the white slopes like a dervish.
Against paddy bird havocking in tall grass,
bluejay, raucous, cardinals
the colour of blood.
For the home-coming catamaran
747 screaming,
wounding the night like a spear.

The monsoon rain
doesn't know me any more:
I am now snowbank child, bundled,
with snot under my nose,
white fluff magic in both hands.
Once, rice and curry, passiona juice,

now, hot dogs and fries,
Black Forest Ham on Rye.

So, what's the essential story?
Nothing   but a journey done,
a horizon that would never stand still.

SR

howdah: the seat strapped to the elephant's back

Conversations with God about My Present Whereabouts

True, I have almost forgotten
the terraced symmetries
of the rice-paddy lands.
How the gods underfoot
churned in time
a golden bowl of rice.
A loss of aesthetics, perhaps.

But I am perfect now.
They have crushed the ears of corn
to feed my belly
white slice by slice
and all imperfections die
with One-A-Day and vitamin B complex.

True, I now walk
without the lumbering skill
of the elephant, the way
he smells the slaughter of mud and hole,
the precision of stars
in his thick legs.

But I am perfect now.
Snow and ice
embrace my horned boots,
skates and skills
the bones uncracked,
the butterfly's muslin wings
untorn among the thorns.

True, I sometimes ask:
Where's the primal scream,
the madness of sun,
the dance of hands and pebbles
by the ocean shore?
And where's the seashell horn,
the words of angels under the sea?

But I am perfect now.
The chameleon
has muted my rowdy scream
to the whisper of a white-boned land,
and stretching in silence,
I am a king of silence.

True, I often miss
the sensuous touch of fingers
on the shying touch-me-not,
the undergrowth's pink badge of bruise,
cacophony of crows,
the rain that pelted my thin bones.

But I am perfect now.
Seduced on shaven grass,
my barbecue glows
like a small hell,
the pork chops kindle,
the Molson cool,
I wear the turban of urban pride.

True, I have changed dead history
to now,
turned my father into me,
the long-gone daddy
now skating on a rink
of clowning children.

But I am perfect now.
I have switched the time and place
of the womb,
my lungs free to scream
though disciplined to whisper,
free to trap the robin in my eye,
if not the strident crow.

I AM perfect now.

A brown laughing face
in the snow,
not the white skull
for the flies
in Ceylon's deadly sun.

EI

touch-me-not: a variety of shrub that closes its leaves when touched

Blind-side Wisdom

No, not a red neck,
 but, let's say, a thick haze
in his searching blue eyes.
 One look at me,
and I'm suddenly afraid of the Biafran sun;
 sees me the next day,
with oiled hair neatly braided,
 gold earring in left ear, a smile
parading four front gold teeth,
 and mistakes me for Derek Walcott
in Carnival mode.
I move next door
 to this other critic,
(who, I learn has never left Ontario
He's out, one day, in his backyard
pruning his apple tree,
 when his eye catches my laundry
fluttering like exotic kites:

saris, dashikis, sarongs, banians
 with pink elephants heavy on the gauze,
bed sheets where the Queens of Sigiriya
 enshrine their mango breasts?
"Hm" The Professor mutters to himself.
 "Definitely one of those . . . I'll bet
he has never heard of Eliot or Yeats
 let along Heaney or Brodsky."

Two young academics
 exchanging notes over coffee at the Inkspot Cafe.
I walk in and order a cappuccino,
 overhear one of them say:
"the guy's a poet. Just ethnic stuff.
 Nothing exciting, not the type
that'll dare piss on the front lawn
 even if the moon is not watching!"

Which is my cue
   to ignore the "Vacant" sign
on the toilet door, walk up
   to the wall with the grand mural
of loons flying over this peaceful lake,
   and piss all over it,
proving once and for all

that what seems is not often so,
   that packaged judgements are like butterflies
that scatter for a sudden wind,
   where even the lion that holds the waterhole
in the face of the raven, slinks away
   when the elephant rumbles in.

New

dashikis: A loose-fitting shirt, often worn in Africa and the Caribbean
banian: cotton vest
Sigiriya: a mountain fortress in Sri Lanka

The Lion and the Crow

Still as stone,
crow lies anaesthetized
under God's gentle hands.
Gone the sheen of sun,
feathers now dull as lead.

Two angels
wearing blue masks
assist in the operation;
ribcage open,
God is in the chambers
of the heart.

"It's bloody and red,
I told you it's red" shouts God
into the accused lion's anxious face;
jungle eyes begin
to squint, mauling paws
go limp.

"Why, why did you do this?" asks God,
a curious but still angry look
in his eyes.
Lion coughs. "He was mouthy,
black and mouthy!
So I pawed him just once.

The arrogant little wimp
tried to fly away,
but I had the loafing wings
well pinned to scrub grass."

"You fool,
who lulls an ant to sleep
under an elephant's foot?
certainly I made crow
bold, black and mouthy,
but also a shimmering shadow
against the sun.

And you   I made
king of the beasts,
though with some severe disabilities:
like getting your wife to hunt
for your meals, an attitude problem,
and far too much siesta
under the acacia.

So, here's the solution:
you, lion, will keep
to the zebra and wildebeest herds,
stroll the waterhole at dusk

like a king, roar
your mouth off as much as you desire,
but   hands off   crow!

I'll instruct
the foul-mouthed prince
to watch his language,
keep to simple domestic gossip,
and stop calling you names.

OK? Bullyboy?"

New

Where Adam First Touched God

Junction. The road forks
like a wishbone.
I choose neither, refuse
the destinies in separate highways.
And so I go for the crotch
of no-man's-land,
the immediate center that seems to belong
to no man, and every man.
Here the division ends,
journey's anonymous oasis
where Adam shall continue
his fallen history.

Where the robin shall sing
with the voice of the paddy bird,
the oak wear the fruit of the jak,
the crows soar with the eagle;
where the dreaming mind
shall have a choice
of coloured snows,

children play with old men,
and the sophisticated young
will again learn their wisdom
from infants, their sanity
from grandfather fables.

I will not travel again
the separate paths of the sun,
the cruel geography of East and West
that blurs the mountain's blue mist,
the green of lush valleys below.
Does it matter which way
the road turns,
there will always be another grail,
another song, another weeping.
Wherever, the wind will never let go
its secrets. Here on undivided ground,
we'll fashion our own mythologies.

SW

Homecomings

Tell me
    of that river
that hugs the monsoon rain,
    takes in the fleeing flood
like a prodigal child,
    smoothes the boulder's jagged face
that juts along its way;

kisses each piece
    of passing driftwood like a blessing;
home to the crocodile's cruising snout,
    primordial jaws, the minnows
that seek the morning sun like a prayer,

and I'll tell why
   there's no frown, no fog
that ever stays over the river's laughing face—
   it knows of home, the journey's end,
where from and where to,
   that the mothering sea   awaits
with pounding heart
   for its prodigal return.

I've meandered
   this way and that,
from shore to shore, one love
   to another, blue skies to cumulus cloud—
under an umbrella of doting children,
   still going   unafraid   laughing,
the blood fevering like some mischievous child—
   always knowing the beginning,
the journey's throbbing walk
   to this igloo of heaven
or that sun-faced island of the elephant
   where I'm always at home,
if not home.

New

The Umbrella of Doting Children

Elegy

Father,
you were a great mathematician,
loved God and the jambu fruit.

You deserve a poem
exact as the sun,
with no beginning, no end,
just an intense line of light
curving to pure circle.

How can I, a child,
trace even a tangent
to your perfect geometries,
the vast afternoons of your brain
in which you walked so easily
with Euclid and Pythagoras?

And how can I compose
that mathematical prayer
of your living, the way
you chased the ultimate equation,
the something that flowed
from heaven to earth,
earth to heaven?

I'll compose
from the genius of my childhood,
use my crayons to draw the perfect tangent
straight to the tip of your tongue:
Ah, the fruit of jambu!
How I shuddered and shook the tree,
and you and I
shared the sweet red pulp
of our mouth's yearnings.

FT

Elegy #2

For Dad

Morning. Black hammering gab of crow.
Trying to tell me something?

Sudden magpie   alone
promising sorrow to wear on my face.

That same night, I heard the jak tree owl hoot
from his darkened throat;

Cats took the parapet wall and caterwauled,
their psalms for the dying.

Father, you died with morning on your face,
fulfilling the prophecies of birds.

I, rocked in the hammock of the sun,
your gentle ways,

refused the dark harbingers,
saw nothing

in the sliced face of the moon,
the broken reservoirs of your heart,

only believed the God
on your wizened face,

your love   now silent
hard as wood.

New

Elegy

For Cleta Marcellina Nora Serpanchy

Dead and not dead.
Gone and here.
You serve breakfast as usual:
hoppers and chicken curry,
coconut sambol, tea in the cold pot.
Talking as you serve, questioning
as you move around the table:
Have you brushed your teeth, child
Washed your face? Done your homework?
Yes, Yes, the answers mumble,
hoppers greater than truth,
half-done sums no match
for chicken curry and coconut sambol.

Yes, I grieve no more, grieve truly:
for grief is nothing without memory
as love is nothing without the proving deed.
Night comes quickly by.
Your small hands lay out our straw mats,
three for your brood of eight;
nor do you forget the daily ritual
of hot milk and Ovaltine for nightcap,
and we close our restless day
with tongues on our saucers like hungry cats.

And how you shaped
the plum promise of Christmas:
Chinese crackers, bundles and bundles of them
tucked carefully in the almirah's bosom;
smell of French polish,
you on your knees squeezing out the shine
from verandah chairs, the red cement floors
a mirror to your sweating face;
the milk-wine bottles preaching
their own sweet vapours.

I gaze once more
at the photograph
with the deep scowl on your face.
You believing truly that rod and child
went together, love held deep
in your small fists. And your cure
for my eldest brother's greed for soda pop?
Immersion theory: 2 cases, one rattan cane,
your hectoring presence,
until he could drink no more,
was duly exorcised.

And me, your immigrant child of the snows?
How in once foolish times
when all hope was gone
and the Afghan moneylender
loomed like a shadow of death
on my threshold,
you threw in the deeds to your house,
your money, your sweet voice of caution:
"Take care, child, take care."

All this,
and how you loved the rose—
with cowdung, bonemeal and crushed eggshells;
the pomegranate tree
always so heavy with promise,
the shoe flower hedge pruned
to a prayer.

Mother, you are dead and not dead.
Gone and here: so the pappadans
crackle on you skillet again,
and you are shouting and chiding,
raving and ranting,   praying,
always praying.   *TL*

pappadans: lentil flour fried and served with rice
hoppers: a kind of pancake made with rice flour and coconut milk
sambol: a variety of salad

Elegy for an Elder Brother

After your death, Hilary,
I saw you flash by in riding clothes,
a whip singing in the air,
boots catching the fire
of the sun.
Hunting? for what?
No quarry, no guns, no dogs,
only cloud and rain
about your ears,

and then I remembered,
I knew: the way
you held your eyes to Heaven,
ran your thin black fingers
over your scientific head
as the runnels of the heart
smoked and clogged
and you muttering the tried mantarams
of your life: Deus, Deus,
O Mother of God,
Thomas, my Doctor Angelicus,
Augustine, beloved sinner and saint,
Hopkins, Merton, Teilhard,
my wounded country, my Decima,
my dear ones . . .

Be still O Hound of Heaven,
the helminthologist, the philosopher,
is dead!
The worm, he always said, belongs to God,
is God,
his sweet obsession, PhD piece
of candy, his metaphor for the good earth,
his perfect passport
to the Academy of Academies.   *RD*

mantarams: religious verse
Decima: Hilary's wife

91

The Quality of Dreams

For Michael

Evening ends his day's mischief like an accident
sharp at 8:30 in the evening.

His brown comforter up to his eyes,
his right hand tight on the fluffy tiger.

Five minutes, and the eyelids flutter
as if in frightened flight,

Chad, the schoolyard bully,
is nipping at his heels again.

Calm returns faithful as a receding wave,
his breathing now disciplined as a clock.

It's the haven of the classroom,
Mrs DeCoo's firm and loving ways.

A smile breaks, something positive
escapes the parted lips,

his small body moves clumsy as jello,
he is playing with Thunderpunch,

the Christmas Tree
is dancing in his dreams.

SR

A New Equilibrium

For Michael

I buy my son this new toy:
a Dukes of Hazard racing tricycle.
His mother protests: "You're spoiling him.
When we were kids we never had

such fancy toys. Only
stick and wheel, old tennis ball,
dirty rag doll, whatever one could fashion
from leaf and crown of coconut tree.
Everything else was imagination, the dream."

So history repeats itself.
Against new wealth we preach old poverty,
against the new profligacy,
childhood dreams in chains.

No ears for either,
my son tears down the driveway,
circling precisely, perilously,
as if to say:

Speed is all, the centre
must now give way to the periphery.
Happiness is in the stirring of the wind
under wheels, the drowning of argument
with a squeal.

SR

Distant Rain

Your exotic pot
of White Rose hibiscus
has never known the Island sun
or monsoon rain.
So memory for you, my son,
is without green history.

As glass and stone
have framed your dark eyes
and all you know
is that land that falls asleep
in soft white pyjamas
with snow flakes to muffle
its heavy breathing,
I guess you'll keep on
asking angrily:
do you have to hang up your story
like a butcher's side of beef?
Why another poem?
Why roll the rock
from the mouth of the tomb,
what's there in shadows, dry bones,
memories?

I raise my tired eyes
from the title of a poem
still new, fierce and lamenting:
"The Rain Doesn't Know Me Any More."
    To remember, to remember
the raindrops
bigger than my childhood eyes,
those blue fists
fast and liquid as a therapist's.

How the good earth churned
its red dust bowl,
burgeoned to batik profusion,

and the sky caught the colours below
like a memory.

BI

Leaving—Michael Style

These are the fractured journeys
of childhood
where the hairline crack
seems wider than a chasm;
where we learn
the true nylon toughness
of the umbilical cord,
how to love
what we think we hate
in the terror of the argument,
hate what we know
is not our mother,
only the genius
of a child's topsy-turvy room,
a set of rioting loafing toys.

So a hectoring voice
once again lays out the charges:
Michael, toys all over the damn place
and they're going
straight into the garbage!

Batman in the dumpster?
Tears drown out the thought.
He makes the traumatic decision.
He must leave . . .

Says so defiantly: I'm leaving!
And mum, cool as tea-country rain,

picks up the gauntlet:
Good. Let me pack your bags!

A sheet of paper
is left behind revealing
a superb map
of his "leaving" itinerary,
his last stop, a legend
that seemed washed ashore
by the tides of the womb:
I WILL BE FOUND HERE!

The anchors hold.
Congenital love survives
the deep frost
as the fires of dissent burn out
by the map's end.
This is a going, a kind of love
that always leaves a paper trail,
that never goes out at all.

RD

My Son

the blood I spilled for you
was real.
For twenty years I waited
at the City gates
for darkness to fall, for stars
to guide my immigrant feet.
Only by dying
do we learn the true rhythms
of the heart, only by crying,
how to laugh from the belly.   *RD*

Baby-Photo Inc vs Michael Egerton Crusz

Five days old
and Baby-Photo Inc got you
in colour, three sizes, and ten copies.
Your father and mother helped
to truss you up in blue "Angel Wear,"
blessed the final shots
with a cheque for $18.50 cents.

But like a small avenging god,
you had grown a sudden fungus
on the Yashica's eye,
bawled your way
to shivering the tripod's thin legs,
bent the picture
to this mere grimace of fists.

Without a choice
of time or place,
they plucked you out
of the flamboyant dream:
how cradled in your mother's arms,
you watched the Temple Elephant
swaying in purple brocade and flame,
carry the sacred Buddha's tooth,
as lean bodies with drums in their heads
jerked between swirling torches,
the evening crowd   hot
with the bloodbeat of Perahera.

And your father
laying you down on that sandy beach
he called Wellawatte,
where once he chased the sand crabs
to their graves,
built castles like some royal architect,
only to have the horizon
collect monsoon darkness like a magnet

and strike . . .

Without the genetic dream,
Perhahera, sand crab, castle,
the drumbeat of your mongrel blood,
of history made, undone,
in some far green island home,
you are no more exotic
than Vancouver crow.

All we have here is counterfeit:
infant bones without marrow,
a rhetoric thin as skin,
the cold eyes of incorporated men,

without blood, without history.

SW

A New Architecture

Song of Myself

How you carved the perfect heart
from raw unseasoned wood,
revealed the dark meat
of the new Caesars, grieved
for the wobble and limp
of small men walking
under cold colonnades;

Used words
to match an embracing kiss,
close a vein,
probe an adamant eyelid,
salve the pain
in a throbbing nerve;

Named the fire
of the undressed sun, the fever
in the eyes of immigrant men;
sang loudly
of elephant and ice, children
pulsing through a continent of snow,
the eagle hovering
in its ether currents.

But have you shared
the pain
in the shattered bird,
the silence
of the thorn that guards the rose?

BI

The Havocking of Silence

How silence,
carried like an infected vein
from the President's Office
an avocado-green memo,
crawled along the hands of the clock
from nine to five,
and fevered walls, carpets,
woodwork, voices,

and I, talkative one,
had to gorge my mouth
with river stones,
sit like an owl in my office chair
and write my homework in the dark.

A winter's mouth
shaped by a prime fist
on my longing lungs,
like a virgin belt
locked, and the key
flung into a manhole.

To havoc
in my sun bones,
where cherubs now show
the stain of blood
on their rice-paper wings
and strum coconut-shell guitars
to hell's red crackle.

I need noise, any noise,
the clap of the sun's thunder
for my green leaves;
I'll take the blare of horns,
stone rhythms from old typewriters,
the swish and scream of women's teeth,
the idiot voices from down the hall.

Or, if you be kind,
let me listen
through these thick walls
to the fervent cry of the peacock,
rain on banana leaves,
or the psalm of blue grass
under my lady's feet,

and I'll remember
that I am still alive.

SW

I Am Now Balancing on Ice
with More Poems in My Hand

For Dad

All agreed
that the omens at my birth were good:
the cow calved within minutes
of my arrival, the caretaker spoke of udders
hanging from a full moon.
The old gardener cried saddhu to the sun
for turning his roses redder than blood,
though he couldn't understand
why their thorns were longer
and sharper this year.
The maid giggled into the verandah
with six warm eggs cupped in her hands,
first offerings
of the black Leghorn pullets.
The family astrologer scaled me in Libra,
promised creative juices
strong as the currents of the Mahaveli.
My mother remarked

that I seemed to have danced in her womb,
and the fat midwife froze
when she slapped my buttocks
and heard my furious cheering
for her expert manipulations.

Only my father was silent,
holding the joy and the torment of the omens
in his eyes,
and, having witnessed the first poem,
silently wondered
when and where, if ever,
I would fashion my others.

EI

saddhu: Buddhist monk

The Disenchanted Child #2

For Michael

Searching her beautiful dark eyes
for gesture   not answers,
my son, Michael, asks his mother:
What's so hot about dad's poetry?

There's more poetry
in your brown eyes,
wave of raven hair,
those small hands
that cook a heaven for our mouths
than all his fancy words
so exotically put together.

And what's so new

about this immigrant theme
that tattoos his work like a woodpecker?
The Red Man is right.
Everybody else is an immigrant.
So we have only a new chart of skin colours:
black and white, brown and yellow,
and all the meti in-betweens.

Is he going mad
for the pot of honey,
forgetting the small potbellied child
he once was
in the green land of long ago?
It's the bubble, the bubble
he romps in, crazy.

Once in the sleepy blood of dream,
I, Michael, sucked the honey
from Milton and Shakespeare,
Blake, Eliot and Yeats,
the Latin boys Neruda and Paz,
the two girls Sexton and Plath:
must have heard the sure sprung rhythm of Hopkins,
Dylan's Welsh rabana beat.

What is left
in the magic of words?
Only the gesture counts.
Like your forgiving eyes
saying gently: Enough, my son, enough.

SW

These Roses Are the Colour of Blood

She opened a vein
and planted a rose,

the thorns she kept
for herself.

In the embrace of the wound,
from bruising and bleeding,

poet and muse
make poetry.

SW

Death of a Poet

I got the word to sing
and the oriole sang,
the mynah bird called,
crow cleared its guttural throat.
You heard nothing.

I got the word to cry,
cry like the peacock
on the trembling brink of rain.
No blood drained your face,
no cry escaped your teeth.

I used the word like a knife
to probe the yellow wound.
You smelled no pus,
no adamant pain,
no crack in the crying skin.

106

I used the word softly
like a baby's milky gurgle.
You held your head stiff,
glued your lips
to your own dark meanings.

I got the word to genuflect,
recite a holy rosary.
You saw no tabernacles
sensed no gods, no saints,
just stared with your cavernous eyes.

And so, you who have never listened
to my green song,
behold the dream:
Me, strangled by my own words
under a brown comforter,
the paramedics carrying
the mangled poem of my body,

and you sitting up
and listening at last.

SR

Poem for the Faltering Man

I'm balancing
on the brink,

death and panorama,
around and below.

But faltering legs,
dangerous geography,

or final decisions
will not make the poem.

Only the supreme electricity
of doubt,

those screaming moments
when wind, muscle and mind

argue
whether to keep me up there,

alive.

New

Libra

The horoscope man
looks at me   floating
under Libra's balancing star
and says to my mother:
HM—

This one
    will surely embrace
the warming word,
    hear the lion roar,
then quickly lie down
    with the lamb.

He'll chase the morning light
    as Apollo   Daphne,
turn away
    from noon's obtrusive red face
and wait
for the twilight hours,
    the raven against a solferino sky,
to play his moods, his poems
    of quiet deliberation.

He'll walk comfortably
    among sinners and saints,
fashion love
    without tragic theatre, touch life
like Beethoven on the keys
    under a haunting moon.

Yes. The poetic juices
    will run, but slowly and sweetly
like the maple's spring sap,
    and in the end,
he'll "go gently into that dark night."

Wrong, my horoscope man.
    For three score years and five,
there's been no balancing act for me,
    nothing in between, no fireside poem
to lullaby the heart, only

hammer and sword,
    bloodstained epaulets
on my tunic;
    fire in a crystal glass, either
the cobra's sac or a love
    that would follow the Christ to Golgotha;

Not for me
    morning's blue mist, only
the sun's tabernacle, the empire
    of high noon; no twilight
when the horizon haemorrhaged
    like a wound,
and the bird in flight darkened its wing
too soon, too soon.

I took the pitch of night,
    with only the winking lamps
of the firefly,
    the solitude, the poem, the jungle theatre
where the elephant   rumbled
    at the waterhole,
and the staccato squeal of the water hog
    was nothing more
than the boisterous order
    of life and death.

No. I will not "go gently into that dark night"
    You'll first hear
the Kandyan drums make fire
    under the dancer's anklet bells,
the raven caw the breaking news,
    the elephant's last clear trumpet—

and I, wearing the skullcap
   of the noonday sun, rosary in hand,
will seek the kingdom of God,
   with the face of a sinner,
and the soul of a faltering saint.

New

Critique in Crystal

"I've read your book: *Elephant and Ice*
with much interest," says the red-haired coed
to the sun-man poet. "I've also seen
your most recent poem: 'The Upside-Down Elephant
Who Would Be a Poet.'
The elephant image seems to rampage
through your work.

"Here's a little something for you,"
handing over a small box
wrapped in sea green paper
with Santa Claus romping all over it.
The silk bow was close
to Indian Ocean blue.
"Thank you," says the poet graciously,
unwrapping the gift quickly
to discover a tiny crystal elephant
basking in the translucent light
of its own body.

Pressing, the poet asks:
"What do you think of my poetry?"
"Look again at the elephant
as it stands on your desk."
He did.

A very lopsided beast
was staring back at him with curious eyes.

BI

... but seek the road which makes death
a fulfilment ... HAMMARSKJÖLD

I will not talk seriously of grief,
or the stabbing moment, or pain
that trickles like blood from under my door.
These I have known, but unprofitably diagnosed
as ugly transients: crows
that permute common dark moods,
angular flights unworthy of netting,
toads croaking for the havoc of monsoon rain
that never happened.

But take this mango leaf,
once a soft green vein of sap
for the honey fruit, a camouflage
styled for safe summer ripening.
Now, cleanly autumned, scarlet,
at the feet of its mother tree,
with the sun veiling its small architecture
like a tabernacle,
and the tree smiling at its roots
for a death
so exotically done.

EI

112

Fresh-cut Flowers

Out there something is laughing
like a chained maniac,
something is laughing
the laugh of the hyena.

Out there something is groaning
with ribs split apart,
something is waiting
for the last mushroom cloud.

Out there something is giggling
in a red pinafore dress,
something is loving
like a frail Mother Theresa.

Out there something is burning
by its own arson hands,
something is crawling
for the last roots of earth.

Out there something is kneeling
before a colour TV set,
something is praying
for the kingdom to come.

The crystal vase
preaches vermilion beauty:

Roses, a baker's dozen, stand
without their rooted hearts,
back to back, thigh to thigh,
face to fragrant face,

cold anaesthetic water
for their feet,
two aspirins by the housewife's grace
to lessen their dying pain.

One terminal rose asks the other:
What is the something out there?

Civilization, they call it,
an art fashioned by the same hands
that have so carefully arranged
our own symmetrical deaths.

SW

The Elephant Who Would Be a Poet

High noon. The piranha sun
cuts to the bone.
Anula, the heaving elephant,
froths at the mouth.
The logging ends.

Without command
he eases his huge body to the ground,
rolls over,
makes new architecture
from his thick legs,
four columns vertical
to the sun.

The confused mahout
refuses the poem
in this new equilibrium,
this crazy theatre of the mind,

this new way
of looking at the real world . . .

SW

114

Going for Broke

I tried Your Trick with a Knife

but cut myself badly,
almost bled to death.
Which proves
that you cannot trust
the people you talk to, admire,
laugh with, read or read about.

How dangerous it is to try
those honoured prescriptions,
without first testing
one's own allergies,

and in the case of poetry
my own penchant
for the profound lie,
the bloodied flotsam
of immigrant men,
the batik and the exotic.

New

These Other Configurations

In a Weathervane Idiom

You talk of fire,
I say arson;
you call it love,
I read lust;
you name it sex,
I hear rape;
you call it neatness
(and say it's next to Godliness)
I suspect mediocrity;
you describe laughter,
I learn the signs of madness;
you call it wisdom,
I see a fool.

Listen to the word
in the soft green womb of the valley,
now shout it
in the rarefied air of the mountain top;
listen to the silence
outside the curved belly
of the woman heavy with child,
now pin your ears to her belly button
and hear the pounding hooves of a new heartbeat,
the hissing waterfall of baby blood.

We embrace words
as we would weapons,
a pin, a shotgun, a machete
for each fighting day.
Until we have words
without fear or favour,
weathervane meanings,
we'll continue to tremble
on our uncivilized arguments of living,
our known condition of death.

SR

119

To Be a Beginner

Resolve to be always beginning
to be a beginner   RILKE

Turn away from the cracked face of the mountain.
For once, try the waters.

Swim. Tingle your skin like fire,
or die, falling and thrashing with bubbles in your mouth.

There'll only be a clasping of hands
(life with death), a soul breaking out of ribs.

All in a flash
you'll learn the language

of new beginnings,
the good earth,

Cherubim and Seraphim
the nether darkness.

What kills for certain
(even before you reach the river)

is the no-no head, the jaundiced skin
that never knows

those other beginnings
how an old configuration can end.

SR

120

A Door Ajar

Everything is green, and the wash
of blue down here, the coral alone
white, twisting its thin warm arms
round my skin.
Air bubbles, globes that burst
to feed my heaving lungs,
have their skins in nothing but gossamer blue.

But I must come up
for air—leave the sharks
curving like lightning in their dance,
their teeth sucking water after
the red ambush of hunger.

Everything is good down here
but we flail our arms
for the blue kingdom of air,
our heads electric
for the sun's nostalgia, the photograph,
the pappadan and ice cream man,
the green land we left
our childhood faces in.

SW

Solitude

Solitude, I love you,
I believe in you, do not betray me   ERNESTO SANCHEZ

This rare moment,
naked to myself, the spinning world,
this deadly brew
that moulds my moods to heaven and hell,
gives mouth to God, stone and tree,
the lamppost woman, the child
with teddy bear in its arms.

This rare moment
when you are mine,
scream from the belly, the hairy head,
show me your madness of laughter,
the blood on your hands;
let the monsoon thunder roll in
the beauty and vulgarity of words.

Give me, again and again,
these rare moments
with which to play the extravagant moods
of men, the farrago world
like a new symphony,
with no man, no world, no me,
ever knowing, ever listening.

SR

Song for the Indian River Man

(Indian River, Keene, 10 May 1986)

For Murray Black

Up river: darkness falls
thick as jute.
Our boat rides anchor.
The cul-de-sac wears its lily pads
like a necklace.
Now here, now there,
the brackish pane cracks and closes,
walleye and bass
electric in their roamings.

A dragonfly reconnoiters.
Mosquitoes sense new summer flesh.
We're armed.
"Off" thick on exposed skin;
a rod in each hand, a net for hauling,
we wear jackets like medieval armour.

No light now but the sky's opening,
a filament weak as a night bulb's.
Darkness abets. We slowly sink
(with bullfrog, lily pad,
the tall wild rice beyond the shoreline)
into the dark hammock
of the river.

Through the evening haze,
I watch the river man's rugged face,
his strong hands the way
he threads his lure, whips his line
like a rainbow's arc.
Soon, a 4-lb small-mouth bass
will fall for his art,
break surface with blood

on his heaving gills.
I often wondered
about the blank spaces of friendship:
his long silences, drifting years,
rumours about his crucible of fire,
how once he tried to walk on water.
What endured? The melody from his old piano,
heady rhythms of guitar,
the wide open spaces of his heart?

Now here he was
fashioning a perfect ecology:
the missing piece in the river's face.
Where else would this man,
ever restless, ever wanting to be still,
find the perfect metaphor?
He was gone. Now only the river,
the dark beautiful night on the waters.

SR

Truth

You called us
    the madcaps,
    idiots with cataracts in our eyes,
    we who dared
    to crawl up the volcano's rib
    and balance on a rim of flame,

who wanted to peep
    into the bowels of the earth,
    test fire
    against the darkness of our limbs,
    the stone in our eyes;
    to listen to the thunder
    of its heart, to learn

the strength of our own rumblings,
when the lava would spill
over the mouth, and brimstone
fall like rain.

And we
who reached the crackling lips,
saw water under burning rock,
felt the throb of power
in our small hands, came back
with salt in our wounds,
a vision of time before history,
a litany of truths
the colour of the volcano's mouth.

And we came back,
still madcaps and idiots,
welts on our climbing thighs,
fire scars on our faces.
But you weren't there
to hear our parables,
read our tablets of stone.

You were dead!

You who drank your tea
from fake china cups, kept warm
with Union Gas air,
your vase of plastic roses
red as the fire
that circled our eyes,
had taken over, each doorway
barred and bloodied with thorns
long as spears.

EI

Don't Worry, Kid, the Wages of Sin is Death

DEREK WALCOTT

Another day.
The Caroni sun shows its face
like a roti of gold
over the cane fields;
and you must rise,
pull on your tattered pants,

make it in time
to the line
where you'll say   amen
to the hoarse voice of roll call;
by noon, the sun will be whipping you
like a runaway slave,

and you cannot hide
your bare back, those throbbing muscles,
the salt in your eyes—
sahib must have his siesta,
and sugar for afternoon tea.

If you ask how or why,
your mother will show
her calloused hands, how
mop in hand   she hunched in pain
over a public lavatory floor
for a handful of rice and beans;
she will tell you why the insurgent rain
fashioned those childhood ghosts
on your tin roof.

And your father?
ask him of beginnings, expectations,
that he found overturned
like a broken lamp
in a burning cane field,
and he'll speak

126

of life and death, the beginning
and the end:
the Carib's cruel prison of birth,
    smell of gunpowder, strange men
    in khaki tunics and knobbed boots;
    how birth is nothing
    But dog days in the sun,
    machete blood on black hands,
    cirrhosis of hot rum,
    how Red Light women
    invade the bloodstream
    like a disease.

Which makes death,
    he would argue,
    not the end
    but the sweet beginning,
    life's first celebration,
    the Angel of Peace
    who sits on your gravestone
    like a blessing.

New

Forever Adam

Alone,
   by yourself,
with only a fly   on the wall,
   naked,
but for a fig leaf,
   hunter
and hunted,

forever cuffed
   to jungle accoutrements:
a carnivorous tooth,
   for the intruder
that slips the raging moon,
   and dares
the waterhole of kings;

eye of the mongoose,
   razor teeth,
the way it tangos
   to the cobra's sway,
then strikes
   with the spasm of lightning;

eagle   wingspan
   a long dark shadow,
the killing beak, claws
   that can pluck
the prairie dog
   like summer fruit.

Don't tell me.
   I know you're Adam
after the Apple,
   with now only a faint echo
of the tempter's voice
   about your ears,
as you balance and dance

on this civilized edge.

But listen,
    I smell it.
I know it's there,
    hanging about the lobby,
sniffing entrances   exits,
    seeking
the red-carpeted stairs
    to your heart;

It has, of course,
    already been in and out
of your fool head,
    as if it were
the honoured guest
    of long ago.

New

Contagion

Is this
    what they call
    the contagion of love?

After they held my feet
    to the palm-leaf fire,
    plucked the amulet
    of a dying God round my neck,
    showed me
    how they flogged an old man
    in a sandpit;

after they spat on my face
    for preaching

the saintly rhythms of the sun,
how it slowly melts its empire
into twilight and shadow, lets shadow
fashion our nights of dream;

life, I said, should sing
    like the morning dove   end
    with the lullaby's sweet amnesia,
    not whine to the engine's smoking burn,
    falter and fall
    to the poison that bears no colour or smell.

So tell me,
    what is the contagion of hate?
    What other masks, snarling faces,
    what new instruments
    will eke out the pain, fashion
    the last wet cough of death?

Will the wound
    still continue to sing in its pus,
    will the spurting blood
    have no redemption?

The weathercocks are spinning
    inthe wind,
    and we, the wise ones
    of cyber space and moon journeys,
    we who sucked the cone
    in a hundred flavours,
    have now chosen to whiz
    by the flaming meteors,
    and cut our paths
    into the dark unknown,
    and beyond!

New

Soul of a Faltering Saint

The Crucifixion—Salvador Dali (1951)

The Spaniard tries to reduce
all human bosh

to the slanting shape of a cross.
Fashions the Christ's head as a gathering mop,

covers our mad history
with a body perfect in its pain

for the moment we bit into the apple,
each time we sent our small world

rolling on its belly.
6
Look again. The pure light

behind the tousled head, over
the brooding shoulder blades,

a kind of effulgence,
the necessary fire.

As for the supreme peace below:
the fishermen, their bleached boat and nets,

that's the other side
of the bloody equation.

SR

Prayer

One season, Lord, only one:
the white slope, skimming, skidding skis,
torches, stars, brandy in the hot chocolate;
for me a demon spirit, pivot, speed,
a descent acrobatic, ether on my face,
for her a smooth curving ride on angel thighs.

No sky with God's fiery head,
rotting fruit, no whirling of leaves,
the maple's stripping tease,
no birthing time, no green mould.
Give me only
the white slope, silent and waiting
for the new architecture of hooves,
the hot fog round my madcap mouth.

SR

Hourglass

You know me, Lord,
in the hourglass of my breathing.
I know you
in your words, your artifacts.

You say, love,
and the face of God
weeps out of the mirror
as if I were a part of the nightmare;
so the Samaritan listens
to the cries in the havocking alley,
and I take to the dank streets
with coffee for hands shaking
out of cardboard shacks.

You say, hate
and yes I see Lucifer
warming his hands
over a dark hellfire, screaming
for a sheaf of light
from the seraphim world;
and I am at it again
planning my ugly menus
of revenge and hate,
how to spin the world
round my cynical dreams.

You say, sing,
and violins coax in
the waking light,
noon   the drums,
twilight   sweet serapina,
night   hot seraglio, lambada,
then utter sleep   silence.

How my world shuttles like a raven
between love, song and hate:
bird now magnificent scythe
against the sun,
now mourning in sweet chorus
for its dead,
then contradictory
as it fouls the siesta air,
or unfurls the skull and bones,
live meat dying in its adamant beak.

Who said the raven
is only shaped to a strident caw,
a sack of black bones
without language or meaning or metaphor?
Who said the bird is beyond poetry,
the hourglass under God?   *BI*

rapina: musical instrument used in Sri Lanka

Sunday Morning

Separate sounds,
church bells and bullets
intersect in the same man;
a black harbinger dog
limps across the Sunday sky.

The old wino's bottle
cries in its dregs,
alley walls soak in his pain,
the wet stones
silently smudge a new grave,
and bodies in Sunday clothes
are slowly moving their limbs to pray.

The sun
without discrimination
warms the forgotten pulse,
the black smoking head,
Christ slumped against a garbage can,

and Sunday clothes
are slowly moving their bodies to pray.

RD

Don't Ask Me What's Happening

Don't ask me
what's happening.

I wouldn't know.

Ask me
what happened,
had happened,
and I'll teach you
how to conjugate life
in the perfect tense.
For I have loved,
forgiven, forgotten,
hated

with a white fire in my brain;
blessed cursed,
laughed and wept
within these four walls.

Seen
the innards
of the heart,
heaven and hell,
here, here,
on this street,
this room, old church
tottering on incense and candlelight.

I have known my God,
adored
when the world was candy and marbles,
questioned, beseeched,
when the dark clouds circled
like vultures.

So, only now am I ready
to let in
the happening thing,
that slice of time
that would dare to balance
on some gypsy's crystal ball,
dance for ever
in the camera's zooming eye.

My past,
those moments of time
I now hold
like a sacrament,
my tempered arguments of living,
epaulettes,
my bloody sword and shield.

BI

Prophecy

When I was a child
and played my happy venial sins
with sunny abandon
in the backyard,
I said, one day, to Jack Jesus,
never, never again,
will I touch the cookie jar
or steal the muffins hot,
and the rooster in the yard
searched my eye
and crowed loudly.

When I became an old man,
I collected my body
and the fleshpots of my youth

and withdrew
to the small cathedral of my soul
to light a candle
to my darkness,
and in the flickering glow
I saw a shape on a cross
and it crowed again

agonizingly.

EI

"Yes, in Our Father's House There Are Many Rooms"

Lord, say: Come,
    I have a place for you here.
I'd like to hear the magic words
    from your Almighty Mouth,
and please, no archangel,
    Burning Bush, sudden revelation
by the broken ankles of a fallen horse.

It's time, Lord, to redeem a promise.
    Your Blessed Mother once assured me
of the Kingdom of Heaven
    if I became a Rosary Nut!
I did, and still recall the night
    I heard the wind bawl out
like a baby,

the apple tree by my window
    convulse in pain,
some hand clamp shut
    the gates of hell,
the night I found my peace
    on earth.

I'm sure she understood my pain,
     saw my face grow dark as beet
as mocking words found their target:
     "Here he comes, fat rosary wimp"
or, "There he goes, Mr Santa Maria Rosary Man,"

hobo who never knew
     the polished touch of mother-of-pearl,
only cheap coloured glass,
     beads with crooked crosses
all so entangled
     that no fingers could quite unravel
these holy knots.

So here I come, O Lord,
     but before St Peter
stamps my passport
     may I ask a few mundane favours?
I'd like my room to be a replica
     of my master bedroom
at 166 McGregor Cres. Waterloo;

A colour TV would be nice
     (preferably a 24-inch)
would help to look in on Colombo,
     Cosby and Matlock,
keep track of what's happening
     in *In The Heat of the Night.*
I almost forgot,
     I'd also like to beg
for some spaces
     for my kids and my good wife, Anne.
So could you please
     change the accommodation
to a small bungalow?

I was also thinking
     (if you don't mind)
of bringing along

my ten books of poetry,
some copies of the "Elegies" I wrote
    for my dad, my ma,
and my brother, Hilary.

I guess, Lord,
    all this might seem
very strange to you,
    but then again not at all.
I know something about
    the Vision of God,
the metaphysical state,
    space without space, time
with no name, legend or end,

but remember?
    I'm right now only in the prison
of my own shapes, the heart,
    the eyes still holding on
to thin glass, seeing
    and not seeing,

the flesh still breathing,
    heaving, the blood as the river
flowing on, and yet
    I wait for your call
that Heaven once promised
    in the small blue beads
of my broken rosary.

RD

The Accepted One

For relics
            a black soutane,
bronze cross
            lying limp
on a breviary.
            Bloodied
with the haemorrhage of martyrdom
in celibacy.

They found
            the cathedral of his cloister
empty:
            Pray, my brothers, they cried,
a priest now walks the earth
                              without
surplice and soul.

Father Magee opened
                        a small door
into a cockeyed world,

and God did not pitch the sun
with dark thoughts.

SR

Small Martyrdoms

Lord, let me pass
    the sackcloth and ashes, the body
that must be whipped
    for the skin to flower
like a bloody rose.

Refuse the saffron robe,
    the Capuchin cowl,
those ancient fakirs
    who would walk the fire, find God
in some cold bare mountain cave.

Don't talk to me of martyrdom.
    Not with my low threshold of pain,
the fool in my head, the beldam hunch
    of the coward. Yes, Peter was impressive
in death, squinting at the Gates of Heaven
    from his upside-down martyrdom
on a Roman cross.

So, could you settle for less?
    Small martyrdoms
from boredom's ugly progeny,
    ordinary chores,
common and necessary as breathing?

I mean dirty dishes,
    chapped hands, fingers
that would scour the pan's dark belly,
    wade daily through Sunlight foam
like some postprandial penance.

I'm moved
    from wall to wall, arching
turning, seeking the dark corners,
    the vacuum's roar
about my ears, an arthritic wince

invading my face.

Come garbage day,
    I'm balancing on the icy driveway,
as the curb   waits
    with civilization's broken toys,
ichor and stink,
    the "Blue Box" brimming
with yesterday's news, Campbell's castaways,
    Kellog boxes,
flat as pancakes.

And when the snow drives down
    like a monsoon rain,
listen to the crack of elbow
    as I strain at the snowblower's starter cord.
No. I'm not smiling
    at the pain in my left clavicle,
the cold wind sneaking through my old parka,
    sputter and smoke,   snow blast
that never fails to find my freezing face.

New

Tramp

After forty years,
this small cloister
seems to hold the face of heaven
in its stone fists,
and Fr. Magee wears his tonsure
like a halo round his greying head.

He now feels the thunder
of bread and water
gushing through his green veins,

144

can call to the brass Christ hanging
on the wall, and the Crucified One
will climb down to him.

Then the stigmata
from cold closing walls,
rituals of midnight prayer,
a leather whip singing
through his saintly bones.

Night.
And he sleeps on his wooden bed
with his God neatly folded
in his black cassock—
suddenly wakes   to a vision:
Francis feeding the birds
from the palm of his hand.

My God, cries Fr Magee,
are you really here,
in this cathedral of stone,
or basking outside with the birds
in the summer sun?

A tramp now walks
a thousand miles,
wraps yesterday's newspapers
against the icy winds,
sleeps with murders, wars and floods
round his cold skin;
babies, whores and policemen
dance like shadows in his dreams.

And old park bench
flings its arms open
to Francis Magee,
and a pigeon
in a skullcap
of flaming red feathers,

coos softly under his limbs.

Tonight,
Francis Magee bundles his God
in a cloak of hemp
and sleeps

in a cloister without walls.

New

"Let us now
in the embracing love of the Father,
Wish each other
The Peace of Christ"—PASTOR MALONE OF ST MICHAEL'S.

So, my brown hand stretches
to the old lady standing beside me.

She turns, glares, extends
a thin pale index finger.

I accept this synecdoche of brotherhood,
and shake hands with a finger,

still believing, still refusing to snuff out
the last candle to our darkness.

New